Moving Beyond

FOUNDER'S SYNDROME

to Nonprofit Success

Thomas A. McLaughlin
Addie Nelson Backlund

BOARDSOURCE®
Building Effective Nonprofit Boards

Library of Congress Cataloging-in-Publication Data

McLaughlin, Thomas A.

Moving beyond founder's syndrome to nonprofit success / Thomas A. McLaughlin, Addie Nelson Backlund.

    p. cm.

ISBN 1-58686-096-8

1. Nonprofit organizations--Management. 2. Chief executive officers.
3. Boards of directors. 4. Executive succession. I. Backlund, Addie Nelson.
II. Title.

        HD62.6.M3918 2008

        658'.048--dc22

             2008009027

© 2008 BoardSource.
First printing, March 2008
ISBN 1-58686-096-8

Published by BoardSource
1828 L Street, NW, Suite 900
Washington, DC 20036

The views in each BoardSource publication are those of its author, and do not represent official positions of BoardSource or its sponsoring organizations. Information and guidance in this book is provided with the understanding that BoardSource is not engaged in rendering professional opinions. If such opinions are required, the services of an attorney should be sought.

BOARDSOURCE®
Building Effective Nonprofit Boards

BoardSource, formerly the National Center for Nonprofit Boards, is the premier resource for practical information, tools and best practices, training, and leadership development for board members of nonprofit organizations worldwide. Through our highly acclaimed programs and services, BoardSource enables organizations to fulfill their missions by helping build strong and effective nonprofit boards.

BoardSource provides assistance and resources to nonprofit leaders through workshops, training, and our extensive Web site, www.boardsource.org. A team of BoardSource governance consultants works directly with nonprofit leaders to design specialized solutions to meet organizations' needs and assists nongovernmental organizations around the world through partnerships and capacity building. As the world's largest, most comprehensive publisher of materials on nonprofit governance, BoardSource offers a wide selection of books, videotapes, CDs, and online tools. BoardSource also hosts the BoardSource Leadership Forum, bringing together governance experts, board members, and chief executives of nonprofit organizations from around the world.

Created out of the nonprofit sector's critical need for governance guidance and expertise, BoardSource is a 501(c)(3) nonprofit organization that has provided practical solutions to nonprofit organizations of all sizes in diverse communities. In 2001, BoardSource changed its name from the National Center for Nonprofit Boards to better reflect its mission. Today, BoardSource has approximately 11,000 members and has served more than 75,000 nonprofit leaders.

For more information, please visit our Web site, www.boardsource.org, e-mail us at mail@boardsource.org, or call us at 800-883-6262.

Have You Used These BoardSource Resources?

BOOKS

Navigating the Organiational Lifecycle: A Capacity-Building Guide for Nonprofit Leaders

Exceptional Board Practices: The Source in Action

Managing Conflicts of Interest: A Primer for Nonprofit Boards

Driving Strategic Planning: A Nonprofit Executive's Guide

Taming the Troublesome Board Member

The Nonprofit Dashboard: A Tool for Tracking Progress

Meet Smarter: A Guide to Better Nonprofit Board Meetings

The Nonprofit Policy Sampler, Second Edition

Getting the Best from Your Board: An Executive's Guide to a Successful Partnership

The Nonprofit Board Answer Book: A Practical Guide for Board Members and Chief Executives, Second Edition

The Source: Twelve Principles of Governance That Power Exceptional Boards

The Nonprofit Legal Landscape

Self-Assessment for Nonprofit Governing Boards

Assessment of the Chief Executive

Understanding Nonprofit Financial Statements, Third Edition

The Nonprofit Board's Guide to Bylaws

Transforming Board Structure: Strategies for Committees and Task Forces

The Board Building Cycle: Nine Steps to Finding, Recruiting, and Engaging Nonprofit Board Members, Second Edition

Culture of Inquiry: Healthy Debate in the Boardroom

The Board Chair Handbook: Second Edition

The Nonprofit Chief Executive's Ten Basic Responsibilities

Chief Executive Succession Planning: The Board's Role in Securing Your Organization's Future

THE GOVERNANCE SERIES

1. *Ten Basic Responsibilities of Nonprofit Boards*
2. *Financial Responsibilities of Nonprofit Boards*
3. *Structures and Practices of Nonprofit Boards*
4. *Fundraising Responsibilities of Nonprofit Boards*
5. *Legal Responsibilities of Nonprofit Boards*
6. *The Nonprofit Board's Role in Setting and Advancing the Mission*
7. *The Nonprofit Board's Role in Planning and Evaluation*
8. *How To Help Your Board Govern More and Manage Less*
9. *Leadership Roles in Nonprofit Governance*

VIDEOS

Meeting the Challenge: An Orientation to Nonprofit Board Service

Speaking of Money: A Guide to Fundraising for Nonprofit Board Members

For an up-to-date list of publications and information about current prices, membership, and other services, please call BoardSource at 800-883-6262 or visit our Web site at www.boardsource.org.

Contents

Preface vii

   A Word on Terminology...vii

   About the Case Studies...vii

Introduction viii

   Founder Characteristics..viii

   The Founder as Employee viii

   The Uniqueness of the Founder's Role ix

Chapter 1: The Founder in the Early Stages.................1

   Two Paths That Shape Leadership Style 1

   Early-Stage Governance Decisions.............................2

   Board Practices for the Next Stage.............................3

   What Founders Can Do..3

   What Board Members Can Do.....................................4

   Case Study 1: The Founder Is the Organization,
   and the Organization Is the Founder 5

Chapter 2: The Founder and Strategy........................7

   Personal Vision or True Strategy?................................7

   How Evaluation Helps 8

   What Founders Can Do...9

   What Board Members Can Do.....................................9

   What Funders Can Do...10

   Case Study 2: The Peril of Vision without Strategy 11

Chapter 3: The Founder and Growth.........................13

   When the Founder Resists Growth despite External
   Demand..14

      Dealing with the Founder's Comfort Level.........14

      How Aversion to Growth Affects Organizational
      Culture 15

      Why Culture Matters, and How an External Focus
      Can Help..15

      Why the Board Shouldn't Ignore Aversion to Growth 16

      What Founders Can Do 17

      What Board Members Can Do 17

   When the Founder Wants Growth at All Costs 18

      How the Founder Can Cause Mission Creep 18

How Staff and Board Respond.................................19

A Subtle Increase in Control 19

Other Outcomes of Growth for Growth's Sake....................20

What Founders Can Do 20

What Board Members Can Do 21

Case Study 3: When the Founder Can't Let Go....................22

Case Study 4: Growth by Lurches............................25

Chapter 4: The Founder's Internal Relationships 29

The Founder's Role in Developing the Board.......................29

The Founder and the Staff....................................30

How the Founder Exerts Influence 30

What Founders Can Do 31

What Board Members Can Do 32

Case Study 5: The Ties That Bind 33

Chapter 5: Founder Succession.................................37

When the Founder Decides to Leave 37

Acknowledgment 38

Severance 39

What Founders Can Do 39

What Board Members Can Do 40

When the Founder Leaves Unexpectedly 41

What Board Members Can Do 42

Firing the Founding Chief Executive.............................42

What Board Members Can Do 42

Case Study 6: A Founder's Luck Runs Out.............................44

Case Study 7: Management My Way............................46

Case Study 8: Strategic Tug of War 48

Chapter 6: From One Founder's Success Story, Wisdom for Other Founders.................................51

Suggested Resources 54

About the Authors 56

Preface

Founders of nonprofit organizations provide one of the most important services in the voluntary sector. They are the ones who must conceive and initiate a process leading to the creation of a new organization almost literally from a blank sheet of paper. Their unwavering commitment, vision, and energy typically drive the organization's growth at an uncertain time. For this they are often well-known in their service area, and their role and accomplishments acknowledged.

Founder's boards of directors don't normally get as much attention. In view of their role this is not surprising, nor is it necessarily inappropriate. But when the constellation of circumstances known as Founder's Syndrome arises, the board must assume a leadership role. Often it is unprepared to do so for reasons unique to the nature of a new nonprofit organization.

The purpose of this book is to speak to both founders and their boards of directors at (or before) a troubled time. With this dual audience in mind, we provide case studies and a narrative of support and guidance that includes two features we call "What Founders Can Do" and "What Board Members Can Do." In this way we hope to help repair or at least help enhance the parties' understanding of their relationship.

A WORD ON TERMINOLOGY

While we use the term *founder* throughout this book, the spirit of our terminology often refers not just to those who found an organization but also to those who serve for many years as its chief executive. For our purposes, a founder can also be a chief executive who has served for the vast majority of a new organization's existence. In most instances, the issues and challenges will be similar.

ABOUT THE CASE STUDIES

The case studies in the book are loosely based on real situations, but the details have been disguised to protect the privacy of the individuals who generously shared their experiences with us. Only the success story in chapter 6 uses actual names of people and their organization.

Although we hope readers will find the situations in the case studies interesting and useful, the real learning comes at their conclusion, where we translate lessons learned into recommendations and tasks for the board and the founder (or chief executive). We hope our ideas will serve as springboards for board members and founders to develop their own creative solutions to the dilemmas posed.

Introduction

We are in the midst of a sustained expansion in the numbers of nonprofit public charities founded in this country. For the last two decades the total number of these organizations has increased steadily, and there is every reason to expect that trend to continue. We believe that this reliable upward trend reflects something profound about founders, their colleagues, and American society. The sheer vibrancy of the voluntary sector is integral to our culture, going back to colonial America when Benjamin Franklin advocated the formation of voluntary efforts to provide everything from firefighting services to the care of widows and children. Today's founders are carrying on a centuries-old tradition.

As a business proposition, the difficulty of starting a nonprofit public charity is far greater than starting a for-profit corporation, and the financial rewards are far lower. While the founder of a for-profit stands a good chance of getting his investment back, the founder of a nonprofit can get only a hearty thank-you, with no hope of ever recovering his donation. Yet visionary founders persist in creating nonprofits.

Why does someone start a nonprofit public charity? There are as many different answers as there are founders, but from our experience we can say that most people who take on this inherently difficult task have a passion for a cause. The word *vision* is overused in the nonprofit sector, but not with founders. Most often they have a true vision, a highly personal, gut-level motivation to do something for others. What they have in mind may or may not appear practical or even feasible, but that doesn't stop them. More often than not they find a way to make it work, even if it means a high degree of personal sacrifice.

FOUNDER CHARACTERISTICS

The one thing that truly distinguishes a founder from her successors is that a founder has to have both a good idea and the capacity to implement it. By contrast, non-founder chief executives need the same (or greater) capacity to implement, but they usually don't need to have the grand idea as well. They are free from the double burden that the founder carries.

Founders in the nonprofit sector also differ from those in the for-profit sector, a difference most traditional business people never really grasp. Why, they ask, would someone so talented and so driven want to dedicate herself to a proposition where the financial rewards are so limited and where the likelihood of daily struggle and possible failure seem so high? We won't pretend to be able to peer inside the mind of a founder, but we will suggest that in response a founder would probably ask, "Can't you see it?"

THE FOUNDER AS EMPLOYEE

There are two other, major differences between founders of successful nonprofits and founders of successful for-profits. The first is that the founder of a large and successful for-profit owns the company. No matter how embedded and beloved a nonprofit leader may become, she can't own the company. The best she can *hope* for is to control it. The distinction is significant.

The second difference is how the leader's tenure ends. Serial entrepreneurs in any industry are rare. The emotional investment demanded by a growing business entity is so high that it is often nearly unimaginable to start all over again. At that point, for-profit founders can usually sell the business. Or, if they take it public, they often become a well-paid chief executive and may very well provide for themselves and their family to a degree far beyond that which most people can accomplish. Gracious living, limitless personal time, and undoubtedly a plush second home await.

By contrast, the nonprofit founder can never be more in the eyes of the law than an employee of an organization that she created. No buy-out offers will beckon, and there are definite limits on the ability to build a handsome retirement package. Besides, passion always trumps a mountain hideaway. With no natural, externally shaped limits on tenure, why step down?

Founders are easy to take for granted. Especially in the early stages, the founder is almost certainly a solo act. Carrying an organization from its beginnings on paper to a functioning entity requires supreme faith in one's self and one's mission. The flaws of the founder-led organization are usually clearest when there is a gap between the founder's past strengths and the current and future needs of the organization. That attractive ability to be resolute in the face of adversity comes to be seen as simple stubbornness. Passion blends into narcissism, and the founder's initial high energy starts to feel to others more like a distraction. Eventually it becomes time for the founder to leave.

The reasons why a comfortable founder might step down, of course, are multiple. The sometimes awkward truth is that simply because someone has founded an organization does not mean that he or she is equipped to lead it many years later. Organizations go through life cycles, and in each one they need different kinds of leadership. Some lucky individuals are able to analyze what type of leadership is needed in each phase of the organization's growth and then find a way to provide it. But in other cases there is a gap between what the founder can offer and what the organization needs.

THE UNIQUENESS OF THE FOUNDER'S ROLE

If all founders adapted to environmental challenges and opportunities this book would simply be about how chief executives lead their organizations. What makes the founder unique is that she typically has extraordinary social and political capital and/or leverage over the board and within the organization due to the intimate nature of a founder's start-up role. As we will show, that capital comes from inescapable steps such as the creation of the first board, the hiring of all initial staff, the shaping of the initial strategy, and the chance to turn a personal vision into a real organization. This capital is built virtually instantaneously, and it represents an unparalleled opportunity in the history of the organization. It takes many forms, the most important of which are implicit trust, deep personal faith in the founder, and the benefit of all doubt. Moreover, many founders are inclined to create a board of directors with strong loyalty to the founder and little experience in being on a board of directors. Any long-serving successor to the founder may very well be able to accumulate the same amount of influence, but almost certainly not in such a concentrated period. To put it succinctly, a founder has extraordinary, long-lasting power.

That capital turns into a liability for the organization when the founder is wrong about something big, because she can still draw almost indefinitely on accumulated goodwill to move in her chosen direction. Most founders run into trouble only when they make a prolonged strategic mistake and cause the organization to deviate from what might otherwise have been a successful path. Even then, they can usually survive on the strength of their political capital alone. In the worst cases, they survive because of the weakness of their board.

The uniqueness of the founder's role — the accumulated political capital of a founder and the likely weakness of the board — is what makes the founder's situation so different when she makes a mistake. In the absence of that mistake, founders' dominant ways would likely go unchallenged. The world of executives is filled with founding chief executives whose domination, petulance, stubbornness, shortsightedness, and other flaws are routinely overlooked because, well, most of the time they're right. That doesn't make their exasperating style or puzzling choices defensible. It just makes it easier for everyone else to overlook them.

For these inescapable structural and cultural reasons, the founder can amass more power than anyone else in the organization, including the board of directors. As long as that power is used effectively and within a broad range of acceptable limits the founder will probably have an unimpeded pathway to the future. When a significant part of the organization's other leadership perceives the founder to have strayed in some major way, the situation known as Founder's Syndrome arises.

For the record, we define Founder's Syndrome as the imbalance of power in a nonprofit organization in favor of the founding executive that occurs because of the unique advantages of assembling the board and staff of the organization. The term is pejorative. No one ever talks about Founder's Syndrome in a complimentary way. We will avoid it in this book because we believe it carries too many negative connotations, as though the circumstances surrounding the creation and early management of a nonprofit organization are little more than a clinical disorder.

Many of the case studies in this publication may seem either negative or slanted against the founder. It is not our intention to denigrate all founders of nonprofit organizations. We present these case studies to highlight an important aspect of this situation: *Without two essential elements — extraordinary social and political capital and a demonstrable long-term mistake or series of mistakes by the founder — the story of the person who started the organization would be no different than any other management story.*

Nonprofit founders typically make tremendous contributions to the public good through the organizations they bring into existence. Moreover, most founders act with supreme good faith in what they believe to be the best interests of their organizations. Their often complicated relationship with their creation deserves a balanced and sensitive exploration that can't be summed up in a bumper sticker. It is our objective to offer that fuller treatment in what follows, and to provide guidance and action steps to make the board–founder relationship a successful one.

1.

The Founder in the Early Stages

In the beginning the founder, the idea, and the organization are one. The founder is driven by passion, vision, and perhaps little more. Creating a nonprofit organization is one of the most difficult tasks in the American economy because the sources of financing are so limited. That makes the nonprofit founder's task even harder and more isolating. Chances are excellent that the founder will for some period be the chief volunteer, the most active board member, the primary funder, and the first staff person.

More important, the founder in this early stage will be the chief cheerleader for the new idea or unusual approach. It is no accident that most founders either have or quickly develop good selling skills. In this stage the founder is marketing a heady mix of the idea, the fledgling organization, and herself. While it is typical and in fact highly desirable for the head of a nonprofit to become its chief booster, the founder often so fully identifies with the organization that it is hard to separate the two. This melding frequently carries on throughout the founder's tenure, and it is at the core of what makes an organization's eventual transition away from its founder so difficult. Latter-stage nonprofits can draw on assets such as a strong brand name, years of trust, and good name recognition, but a founder-led organization has none of these advantages and so must necessarily draw deeply on the personal qualities of the founder for early success.

TWO PATHS THAT SHAPE LEADERSHIP STYLE

There is another critical aspect of the newly founded nonprofit organization that dominates early-stage decision making by the founder and therefore shapes her leadership style tremendously. We think of it as prototype creation. Nonprofit organizations can spend most of their time creating and managing a prototype model of service, or they can mass-produce (industrialize) a well-known and accepted service. Prototype organizations are usually small and/or new entities, whereas industrializers tend to be large and well-established entities producing large quantities of the same kinds of services.

Nonprofits follow one of these two paths because they are usually started in response to the founder's perception of some kind of dysfunction in society. Whether it is a need for health care, education, adoptions, broadened access to world-class art, the prevention of environmental catastrophe, or a thousand other matters, the nonprofit exists to solve problems that the commercial or governmental arena can not or will not address. But when you are the first in the country or at least your region to attempt to resolve a problem, the initial reality is that *neither you nor anyone else really knows what needs to be done or how to do it*. As a result, one has to create prototypes first to see what works best.

For example, when the AIDS crisis first appeared in the 1980s, no one knew very much about the disease, the people who suffered from it, or exactly what practical things they needed. As a result, the initial period was a repetitive cycle of research, experimentation, and evaluation until treatment methods and appropriate support systems were designed and implemented. Even when the nature of the service the founder is trying to provide is clear, there is still an almost inevitable period of experimentation before the organization attains the best mixture of program model, management systems, and revenue sources.

Almost all founders must of necessity create their organizations as prototypes. If the idea is right and it is marketed effectively, the organization can grow indefinitely and may eventually become an industrializer. Often, founders will look back at the prototype years as the most exciting period of their new organization. The adrenaline rush of a fast-paced environment, the sense of exploration and discovery, and the early confirmations of success are enormously stimulating and even addictive. In that context, the founder can perhaps be forgiven for acting "as if she owned the place" and for making snap decisions that aren't always textbook-correct. That doesn't make this behavior admirable, just understandable.

EARLY-STAGE GOVERNANCE DECISIONS

Naturally a founder will draw board members, early staff members, and donors from like-minded friends and colleagues. This tendency only makes sense, because one builds a future on strengths, and a social network is a good source of strength. What is less apparent at this stage is the possibility of a subtle short-circuiting of the ideal board–chief executive relationship because of the personal ties to the founder that may predate the board member's involvement with the organization. Legal and nonprofit organizational theories hold that a board member has a fiduciary duty to the entity. Inherent in this belief is a kind of arm's-length relationship that provides a fundamental formula for accountability. But the founder's board is more likely to feel a stronger duty of loyalty to the founder herself. This connection is an endless source of political capital for her.

Political capital can have a dominating effect in the early stages of a nonprofit's history. Not only is it dominating in and of itself, but since most start-up nonprofits are small organizations, the founder's political capital overwhelms the culture. Years later, if the organization grows substantially, it would take a highly driven and unusual leader to exercise such dominance. The founder can do so almost without trying because of the small size of the entity.

In private for-profit companies there is often a tight fusion of ownership and management by design. Some tax laws even encourage the formation of business structures that deliberately blend personal and organizational interests for tax purposes. But the difference between management's personal interests and corporate responsibilities could not be clearer than in the nonprofit sector: They can never be identical. One of the most difficult things for the founding board to understand is that it is the responsible body for the organization. It is necessary to work in harmony with the founder, but it is also important to realize that there is a line between governance and management. The sooner the board learns about its specific role in the organization, the easier it will be during the coming months and years to develop a healthy relationship with the founder.

BOARD PRACTICES FOR THE NEXT STAGE

Fortunately for the founder, in this early stage the board's loyalty is rarely tested, largely due to the singularity of purpose and the blending of personal and institutional agendas centering on the founder. The sense of united purpose is strong now, and if one were to ask about this potential tension the question would almost certainly be dismissed as irrelevant or silly.

It's not. A tax-exempt status is based on trust between the public and the entity, and it should be treated accordingly. What obscures the question is the organization's small size. A start-up nonprofit in the prototype stage is a bit like a small club, open to the public in many ways but fundamentally a product of a small network of relationships. It doesn't necessarily intend to operate as a closed entity, but the intensity of the work and the small scale can make it seem that way.

If a nonprofit grows in size and learns how to mass-produce its services, it will find that that kind of cliquishness tends to change on its own. With a larger, complex entity, it is difficult to maintain a closed inner circle even if that is desired. Of course, many nonprofits never grow much beyond the prototype phase. There are more than 1.6 million nonprofits and a little more than 1 million of them are public charities. According to the Urban Institute's 2007 report, about 60 percent of these charities have revenues of less than $250,000, suggesting that they are classic prototype organizations.

There is a tendency for board members of a start-up to feel a certain sense of gratitude to the founder, not only for being included in such an interesting venture but for investing so much of herself in the task. This attitude is normal, but it can impair board members' judgment. It may be a tiny speck on the landscape now, but that valiant little start-up organization (and its founder) could some day be giants. Better to adopt good practices now rather than try to reform them into existence later on.

WHAT FOUNDERS CAN DO

When founders feel like they've been carrying their organization on their backs, chances are that's exactly what has been happening. They really are the heart and soul of their organizations. That is both good and bad. The good part is obvious. The bad part is that every organization has to grow to the point where it can exist separately from those who created it. This was the case for Katie's Story, the organization described in Case Study 1, "The Founder Is the Organization, and the Organization Is the Founder" (see page 5). Founders can take these steps to share their burden:

1. **Build systems based on the organization's way of doing things.**

   Strong systems can carry on no matter who serves in chief executive or staff roles. Admittedly, founders may feel frightened when considering the organization without them at the helm. But this feeling may dissipate when they realize that without systems that serve as bridges to the future, their legacy might be "She created a great organization; too bad it fell apart after she left."

2. **Prepare the board to think and act on its own, independent of the founder or chief executive.**

The board should have its own systems, benchmarks for success, and ability to monitor and propagate itself. This doesn't mean the chief executive has become merely an interesting advisor, because a well-constructed board can do a lot to amplify the passion and the vision of the chief executive.

3. **Coach and teach.**

There are probably many people working in the organization now who weren't there when it was founded years ago. Leadership by example is laudable, but founders have to find ways to connect with more people more quickly now that the organization has grown and to impart the wisdom they acquired the hard way.

WHAT BOARD MEMBERS CAN DO

Boards of directors may be tempted to stand back and let the founder take over. After all, this was her idea, she has the commitment and the energy, and in any case this is a part-time undertaking for board members. This is understandable, but misguided. The proper course has to be set from the beginning, and just because the founder has many admirable qualities doesn't mean that board members should ignore their fiduciary responsibilities.

1. **Insist on written policies and procedures, and work with the founder to create them.**

2. **Make meetings matter.**

   Set a good example by ensuring that meetings have stated objectives, an agenda, and someone to take notes or formal minutes (as appropriate). Follow up on action items.

3. **Shape a board that works.**

   Pay special attention to the creation of the nominating committee or the board member nominating process. This committee should seek out board members for what they can offer the organization in the future, not for their relationship with the executive.

4. **Build a board team.**

   Work at getting the board to operate as a team independent of the chief executive. This means that each board member should have a clear grasp of the board's responsibilities, values, procedures, and strengths. It is also a good foundation for holding the chief executive accountable in the future.

5. **Look outside the organization.**

   Make time to talk extensively with the organization's network of community leaders and potential clients so that you can lay the framework for short-term planning.

6. **Return to #1 and revise continually.**

   Successful practices will inform improvements to initial policies and procedures, so be prepared to revise constantly based on experience.

~ Case Study 1 ~

THE FOUNDER IS THE ORGANIZATION, AND THE ORGANIZATION IS THE FOUNDER

When a nonprofit leader cannot distinguish herself from her work, she will find it particularly painful as the organization begins to adopt its own identity. How can the board help founder Mary Meyer and her husband Phil through this challenging period?

When Mary and Phil Meyer's only child Katie passed away from cancer in 1985, the idea of starting a nonprofit organization was the farthest thing from Mary's mind. But when her best friend offered a grant from her family's foundation, Mary decided to found Katie's Story as a way to memorialize Katie while channeling her grief into a positive purpose.

Mary was convinced that other parents would be grateful for the opportunity to learn how she and Phil had negotiated the U.S. health care labyrinth to get the best care possible for Katie during her long illness. Mary's theory proved to be correct, and for several years she made guest appearances in the Midwest and, eventually, throughout the country. The speaker fees accumulated, while contributions to Katie's Story poured in from all parts of the country after Mary's appearance on the *Oprah Winfrey Show*. Katie's Story became synonymous with Mary's story. Mary's life took on new meaning.

In time, the bookings for Mary's appearances slowed and then ceased. Luckily, the board had prudently invested a portion of the incoming funds during the early years, even as they awarded grants to families burdened with cancer-related costs.

Now a majority of the board felt the organization needed to revisit the mission and organizational name and to rebuild the funding base. With the emergence of the Internet, many thought it was time to focus efforts on facilitating Web-based communications among parents, which would not necessarily require Mary's involvement as the central figure. Several board members also wanted to sponsor regional cancer-care conferences featuring expert health practitioners and patient advocates. They believed funding from institutional sources would be available to support these purposes, and individual support in the form of contributions and memberships could come from a select group of parents and other friends.

Mary, who served as board chair as well as chief executive, was devastated. She couldn't believe the board would betray her like this. Her husband Phil, also a board member, chastised other members and spoke out on his wife's behalf, suggesting that the board sponsor a new multistate tour that would once again feature Mary as guest speaker. He challenged board members to allocate additional dollars to marketing this time around and reminded them that, after all, one of their primary responsibilities was to ensure adequate resources for the pursuit of the mission.

Tip for the board: *Lead the organization while supporting Mary in her changing role.*

The board is on the way to making the right decision for the organization, and it must continue to move in this direction. It's important to examine this situation from two perspectives: the board's responsibility to lead the organization and Mary's emotional investment in this organization.

First, the business side: An organization is more than one person. Mary is a headliner who can serve many different purposes, but she does not constitute the whole mission. While this job has been good therapy for her, she did not create a sound organization. Now the board is correct in betting that a very different program model may rescue the organization. Mary needs to embrace this new direction — and in the process reinvent herself as an anticancer activist — or she needs to disengage.

Second, Mary's emotional health: The board is not responsible for it, but this shouldn't stop members from feeling enormous empathy for her. She will need the full support of the board to accept the new direction and her role in it, and the board should provide it. With the evolution of her role, she may initially feel as if she is reliving the loss of her daughter. But the board must remember one thing — it has a duty of loyalty to the *organization*, not to Mary or to Mary's husband — very little good can come of putting a chief executive's spouse on the board of directors.

Tip for Mary: *Put the organization's needs first.*

Mary should congratulate herself on creating this organization. Bringing together so many passionate people is a tremendous accomplishment. This must make what just happened doubly difficult to understand. However, having gained strength and inspiration from their experiences in working with Mary, the board of directors is taking the organization in a new direction, and they are probably right. They understand that the recipe for success changes frequently in the nonprofit world and they are trying to get ahead of that change. This is not something that Mary should take personally.

The board didn't reject *Mary*, it rejected a plan that continued to count on Mary as the primary fundraiser and the face of the organization. It is understandable that Mary took this decision personally, though. As the founder, the distinction between her and her organization was blurred. Mary and her husband need to understand that this was the best decision for the organization, even if it's not the best decision for them.

Mary needs to find a way to get behind this new direction. Doing so successfully will aid her personal and professional growth considerably. It's good that the board didn't terminate her, but she needs to remember that as long as she is part of this organization she is an anticancer activist first, and Mary Meyer second.

2.

The Founder and Strategy

Strategy is about the future, and it is about choices. It is an intellectual overlay that we devise to impose a present-day guide on the uncertainties of the future. The best strategies operate like shared personal compasses that give a nonprofit's leaders a way to pick their way through the distractions and noise of everyday events. In a well-run, mature organization, the strategy is widely understood and accepted, often because the process of developing it was inclusive enough to build a broad base of support. But a founder's new organization has none of those advantages. Almost inevitably, the initial strategy comes straight from the founder's creative mind. Also almost inevitably, the strategy works.

This pleasant outcome can establish an unfortunate pattern. What many founders actually have is a vision, not a strategy. The two can seem quite similar, but a vision is a visceral, individualized experience, while a strategy is based on a shared understanding of the organization's future environment. In addition, a personal vision is usually a source of passion and energy, while a strategy is necessarily more cool and calculating. No founder is ever likely to feel that her vision is based on facts and realities — but a strategy must be.

The founder probably started with a vision long before the strategy evolved — if it ever did. And often that vision can carry both the founder and the organization through many years. But eventually the organization grows too large or too old for that fresh vision to endure. Succeeding generations of board members and employees don't instantly share the vision, and they may not even be aware of it. This is one reason why some founders prefer to keep their organizations small. Small nonprofits are more readily governed with an emotional vision because it can be communicated individually to everyone who works there or serves on the board. Larger organizations are always governed by a strategy, even if it is piecemeal and/or poorly communicated, because passion can only penetrate through so many layers of employees.

PERSONAL VISION OR TRUE STRATEGY?

Founders will get into difficulty if they cannot transition their vision into a strategy that the rest of the organization can understand, or if they try to exert leadership through vision or passion alone in a large or growing organization. Most nonprofits — indeed, most individuals working in any entity — appreciate the regularity of a defined task, an established approach, and predictable outcomes. When the predominant leadership guide is a personal vision in place of a true strategy, none of these things are possible. (Case Study 2, "The Peril of Vision without Strategy," on page 11, shows what can happen when a personal vision outruns the institution and its established strategy.)

If the founder does choose to draw guidance solely from her personal vision, the result may be that everyone else sees an increasingly arbitrary, unpredictable leader.

Hunches and impulses — but only the founder's — are likely to scramble the topography of leadership. The lasting damage comes not from whether the founder is right or wrong but from the maddeningly inscrutable style of leadership. To succeed, organizations need culture, strategies, management systems, and networks. What all of those things have in common is that they are the products of people working together, not the products of solo acts. Management consists of getting things done through other people, and the founder who cannot get outside her passion will have a hard time managing.

When a founder struggles in this way, the frequent result is a "trust-me" culture. Trust is in many ways the currency of nonprofit organizations, so perhaps this is why the founder can get the benefit of the doubt for so long in the absence of a successful strategy. After all, she has already been proven right at least once by virtue of the existence of the organization, so who's to say she's wrong now?

Other confusion arises if a founder is allergic to strategy. When the passions and personal visions of a single individual lead an organization, the future tends to look like "The New Exciting Thing." This category can be occupied by virtually anything — a new program, a prospective donor, a new board member, a compelling idea, a promising practice from another part of the country, and so on. Whatever that "thing" is, it is likely to be red hot for the moment, and it will suck the oxygen right out of any attempt to focus on what, by contrast, will seem like the boring details of leadership. It can also allow the founder to keep control of the agenda and crowd out inconvenient matters. Note, however, that allergy to strategy is probably a genuine tendency of the founder's, not a cynical technique to avoid dealing with certain things. Remember that the founder really is excited by all the possibilities.

How Evaluation Helps

If a founder operates without a clear strategy understood by all, there can be no real accountability for her decisions and choices. Sometimes the lack of an evaluation mechanism for the chief executive is evidence that strategy is missing or unclear. In all fairness, most organizations and many people find any form of personnel evaluation uncomfortable to give and threatening to receive. Nevertheless, the leaders of tax-exempt organizations have a moral as well as a practical responsibility to establish just such a system (and the chief executive has the responsibility to establish the same system for the staff). In Case Study 2, "The Peril of Vision without Strategy," an evaluation would have helped to identify Ian's restlessness and encouraged Ian and the board to explore new ideas that would benefit the organization.

The board is specifically charged with completing this kind of evaluation. This is, of course, the same board that the founder probably hand picked and maybe even begged to sign on at the start. Add to that the tendency of nonprofit board members to seek unanimity and avoid conflict, and you have a prescription for inaction.

What Founders Can Do

Founders start organizations out of sheer excitement and carry them forward on determination and adrenaline. But as organizations grow and mature, they need a different kind of leadership.

1. **Get to work on strategy.**

   Founders separate the tasks of creating strategy from the day-to-day needs of the organization. It's easy to become so wrapped up in those pressing needs that creating a strategy seems like a distant dream (or nightmare). There are plenty of great articles and books on strategy to help founders get started.

2. **Make your strategy known.**

   Some founders think they have a strategy, but it is only in their heads. If their closest colleagues don't know for sure what the strategy is, then the organization doesn't really have one.

3. **Involve board and staff.**

   Both need to be part of the process of creating a strategy. Hiring an outside facilitator may make the process run more smoothly and help eliminate confusion about roles.

4. **Appreciate the benefits.**

   Done properly, strategic planning is a powerful exercise. It helps people shape the future of the organization. This may be the first time the founder has shared so much power with others in the organization and it may be uncomfortable at first. It may help founders to remember that power multiplies when it's shared.

What Board Members Can Do

Assuming the organization is too small to have a significant number of senior managers (who are better positioned to insist on a strategy), the board of directors needs to exert a substitute form of leadership. The objective is to develop a written, internally understood statement of strategy. The difficulty is almost certain to be that the founder will resist the effort.

1. **Take the initiative.**

   One or two board members should begin by saying something like, "Everyone sort of knows our strategy, but let's try getting it down on paper to make sure that we're all working with the same understanding." Sometimes the problem is not the absence of a strategy, but the absence of a strategy that is well communicated.

2. **Involve the founder.**

   Spend considerable time interviewing the founder, her managers, and other internal leaders to intuit the strategy that the founder is unwittingly carrying in her head. Especially in the beginning, the founder may well be right about the correct strategy.

3. **Begin a strategic planning process.**

   As a more formal approach, initiate action at the board level to begin strategic planning. The founder will probably resist this top-down effort, too, so board members must build a coalition of like-minded board leaders and be persistent with the founder until she relents and a process can be developed.

WHAT FUNDERS CAN DO

Funders are in the best position of all to stimulate the expression of strategy, especially those who have funded the organization before. *Funders* tend to be institutional suppliers of significant funding in the context of a relationship, while *donors* tend to make smaller and possibly only one-time contributions. Funders often have influence by the sheer volume of a single contribution, while donors only have influence if they somehow can act in concert with each other (such as in federated fundraising).

1. **Point out why strategy is important.**

   While praising what the founder has accomplished, institutional funders can explain the many benefits of having a clear strategy. If necessary, they can even make it conditional in some way.

2. **Practice strategic grantmaking.**

   Funders should offer funds for the organization to do what they want it to do. This near–trump card is a funder's best chance at stimulating an organization to create and communicate a clear strategy.

~ Case Study 2 ~

THE PERIL OF VISION WITHOUT STRATEGY

Highly successful nonprofit founders who survive many organizational transitions may come to believe their boards will go along with any new direction they might suggest. Should the board support Ian Venable's new plan to significantly expand the nonprofit's service area?

The nonprofit founded by Ian Venable had delivered excellent and highly successful workforce development programs in Jackson, Miss., and surrounding areas for more than 20 years. Ian's board, which consisted of members from the region, admired Ian and always gave him the highest ratings during his annual evaluation.
A skilled fundraiser as well as a talented leader, Ian operated the organization in the black and secured an endowment of $30 million, primarily from non–board supporters.

After Hurricane Katrina, the restlessness Ian had felt for some time intensified. He had been doing the same thing in the same place for what seemed like an eternity, and, frankly, he was bored. Meanwhile, there was great need in the New Orleans area — not to mention the countless millions of dollars flowing into the region. For weeks, Ian fantasized about moving to New Orleans and helping the city rebuild; then he decided he must act. He developed a written transition plan that would take his nonprofit, its new programs in urban development, and a significant portion of its endowment to the heart of the action in Louisiana, with the board expanding to include majority representation from that state. The organization's workforce development programs were destined to become secondary initiatives managed by a satellite operation by the end of three years, according to Ian's plan.

Ian introduced the plan to his board at a special meeting. Following his presentation, he was asked to leave the room while the board discussed the plan. When Ian returned, he was shocked to learn that the group that had always supported him in the past was no longer willing to follow his lead. He could not believe that the board chair — a close friend as well as an associate — was telling him that if he was determined to pursue his new plan, the only option would be for him to resign and start a new nonprofit.

Ian had labored for years, running a nonprofit of incomparable quality and raising a hefty endowment without taxing the board financially, and this is the thanks he got?

Tip for the board: *Stand firm, and repair communication.*

Ian is off base here, and the board is right to tell him so. Ian would be wise to do exactly what the board suggested — start a new organization. Ideally, he'd do so with the full knowledge and consent of the board of directors, which could ultimately feel good about spinning off an idea that was too important to constrain. The other useful thing board members could do at this point is to examine critically how such a big idea could have gotten so far without them and to ask themselves if they need to improve lines of communication between the chief executive and the board.

Tip for Ian: *Change course, and do it the right way.*

Ian may be restless and looking for something new, but that doesn't mean that the organization should follow his lead. If this were a for-profit organization that Ian owned, he would be perfectly within his rights to uproot and move the entire entity. But it is a nonprofit and Ian is the founder, not the owner. There is a larger loyalty here beyond personal interests, no matter how well-intentioned they might be.

This is also potentially a legal matter. Many aspects of nonprofit public charities are regulated by state laws; an enduring principle behind such regulation is called *cy pres*, a Latin term meaning "as near as possible." This organization's funds — and the assets they purchased — may very well be inextricably tied to workforce development in Jackson, Miss., and cannot legally or morally be transferred to another city in another state, no matter how deserving.

What Ian wishes to do is laudable, and he should be encouraged to do it. But he will need to do it the same way he founded his first organization — from scratch. His board is right, but its intent is not punitive. If Ian is going to change course, he has to do it the right way.

3.

The Founder and Growth

Nothing is as important to the growth of a nonprofit organization under its founder as the long-formed ideas the founder carries in her head. Even powerful outside influences can pale in comparison to the ideas about growth, size, scale, and complexity from which the founder operates. On occasion this mental model is clear to the founder and her colleagues, but most of the time it is not. But it usually exists, and it profoundly shapes the organization.

Founding a nonprofit organization is an act of hope and confidence. No matter how much research and planning have been done — and frequently there is little of either — the founder is making a profoundly emotional statement about what she hopes to do for society and her confidence that it will actually happen. This blend of hope and confidence is often no different from those who found a for-profit organization, but since the prospect of substantial riches arising from the founding of a nonprofit is dim, the real payoff is in emotional currency.

In the beginning, founders have to operate from the gut. Starting with the simplest decision, such as who should be on the board or who should be hired for the first jobs, the founder usually doesn't have a team of trusted advisors to rely on. Judgments have to be made quickly, and there is little time to ponder short-term implications, let alone long-term impact. The founder is in ready-fire-aim mode all the time. From this early period emerges what turns out to be her tremendous internal political capital.

For all its stress and uncertainty, the first years of an organization can be an exciting time. Once the wheels start rolling, the cascade of planned and unplanned events, rapid-fire decisions, bursts of self-discovery, and sheer stimulation make it a period of high adrenaline. And the founder is undeniably at the center of everything.

This period is significant because the future of the organization is being silently shaped. Even the smallest decision builds on the ones before and makes some future choices more likely while restricting others. Since most founders carry the strategy in their own minds long before putting it to paper or working it through with the other leaders, that strategy — however finely or poorly shaped — is the only possible unifying force at this stage.

The founder's choices in relation to the logic of external demands can set up a conflict for the organization. If the choices are appropriate within their strategic context, the founder's attention can turn to issues such as personnel management, relationship with the governing board, and so on. But when the founder's chosen pathway deviates significantly from a broad but strategically logical direction, tensions grow from within.

This internal conflict becomes problematic in one of two ways:

- The founder's resistance to growth keeps the organization small in the face of external demand.

- The founder wants growth at all costs.

WHEN THE FOUNDER RESISTS GROWTH DESPITE EXTERNAL DEMAND

There are many legitimate reasons for keeping a small organization small. Sometimes there is no real alternative because the demand for services is so limited. At other times, the external environment signals a need for more services. When services to the mentally ill and developmentally disabled were shifted from an institutional model starting in the 1970s, for example, there was a steady demand for more nonprofits to run community-based programming. Changes in federal funding at the end of the 20th century resulted in a demand for more education-based after-school programming. In these situations, even a casual observer could read the signs that society approved of the services already being provided and had decided it wanted more. Organizations that responded grew significantly in a relatively short time.

As with any market, suppliers who refuse to meet the demand facilitate the growth of competitors. Those competitors may start out looking like the founder's organization, but over time in a growing market, there is a clear divergence. The founder's organization tends to stay in that early excitement phase of innovation and discovery. For example, visiting nurse associations a century ago essentially invented the modern home care model, but many remained locally focused and small. They left an opening for for-profit home care services, and eventually visiting nurse associations surrendered their dominant market position to national for-profit home care chains.

DEALING WITH THE FOUNDER'S COMFORT LEVEL

Faced with a demand for growth, some leaders shrug it off, citing any number of legitimate reasons: fear of future funding cuts, concern about the organization's ability to deliver the larger number of services, or a sincere conviction that small service units and small corporate entities are always the best approach. A founder gets into difficulty if the real reason for refusing growth is a personality preference for remaining in an established comfort zone, not an approach based in serious strategic considerations.

The slow erosion of the founder's initial strategic position as a leader is deceptive. Even modest growth can lull the leadership into a feeling of keeping pace with change, though others are growing at a much greater rate. Through passionate conviction the founder can hold that small is beautiful and that nonprofits are meant to be synonymous with local, community-based initiatives. But in reality the founder has reached a kind of set-point with the organization, a balance between external demand and internal capacities. She simply is not comfortable taking the organization to a new level.

This idea of comfort should not be underestimated. The founder with this kind of mental model of success may prefer the intimacy of a small organization. Not only does everyone know everyone else's name, but they know a fair amount about their co-workers as well. The term *family* as it applies to a workplace is overused, but that's not far from what this type of founder desires. The pleasure of affiliating with a defined group of like-minded co-workers is a large part of the pleasure of the job.

HOW AVERSION TO GROWTH AFFECTS ORGANIZATIONAL CULTURE

Relationships become of primary importance as productivity and program accomplishment are taken for granted. The entity may have started out with a strong focus on the consumer and the vision, but over time it becomes inward-facing. The culture becomes self-referencing, and the circle closes to outsiders (which may include funding sources). In the absence of an external challenge — which probably won't come because funders will take their new money elsewhere instead of challenging their existing recipients — the operation becomes stunted and immune to change. A similar progression of events leads to a situation in which the founder can't let go. (See Case Study 3, "When the Founder Can't Let Go," on page 22.)

If the founder who resists external demands for growth is guilty of anything, it's a sin of omission. No one can fault her for not pursuing opportunities, and the insular nature of the culture tends to obscure them anyway. The board is pleased with the founder (name three good reasons why they shouldn't be), and there may even be some level of outside approval. No one can truly find anything to argue with here — except funders. Funders feel the full range of the dysfunction they have asked the founder's organization to help solve, and they feel a sense of urgency about building a widespread solution. When an organization proves unwilling to provide a solution, they know their best option is to simply leave. Additional funding either comes sparingly or not at all.

WHY CULTURE MATTERS, AND HOW AN EXTERNAL FOCUS CAN HELP

The impact of a culture like this one is subtle: The founder and her employees are being nourished, but the entity is not. As a result, only a board member or employee who is interested in the larger strategic environment is likely to be in tune with the messages that the environment is sending. This pre-existing interest may have brought them to the organization in the first place, so they have an expanded channel for information and input.

These externally focused board members and employees can be found, for example, in nonprofit service entities that arise from successful advocacy — such as organizations serving developmentally disabled individuals, which emerged in the middle of the last century. In the process, some advocates themselves became founders and managers, but because their pathway into management originated in advocacy, they were more likely to remain connected with loose networks of advocates and to have their own historic perspective on the services needed.

When a founder has a small-scale orientation, one of the likely evolutionary stages for the organization is that those with an independent understanding of the larger external need and sympathy for the issue will, over time, self-select themselves out of the group. This is one of the ways early founders in a particular need-area end up creating the next generation of founders — and their own eventual competitors.

WHY THE BOARD SHOULDN'T IGNORE AVERSION TO GROWTH

How does the founder who prefers to keep her organization small in spite of rising external demand for its services remain in place? The answer is rooted in the nature of the founder's social and internal political capital. First, many board members and employees tend to think that "big organizations are impersonal" and "small is beautiful." Employees without a strong interest in the larger environment are more attracted by the inherent appeal of the work than by whether the founder is keeping pace or not. But the ultimate source of staying power is that being a founder provides an almost permanent benefit of the doubt. Board members are aware of what the founder has done, and they often feel it is disrespectful to appear to question it. Besides, she's always been right up to this point, hasn't she?

In the end, the founder with the aversion to growth generally has every opportunity to create a small, perfectly respectable functioning organization that will continue as long as funding sources can be found for it (interestingly, the more market-driven the funding, the less likely the growth-averse founder will prevail). Mostly she risks irrelevance for her creation and a kind of permanently quaint status for herself as peers grow, mature, and develop. This is hardly a prescription for professional or organizational catastrophe.

What it does mean is that the founder creates an organization that fits her like a personally tailored suit, and she operates that way indefinitely. Things work as long as there is no significant challenge (such as a strategic threat or a boomlet of opposition on the board). When this type of founder leaves the organization, major change usually follows. Succeeding a long-term chief executive is never easy, and rarely can the organization avoid considerable upheaval with a new leader, even if it is temporary.

But by that time the new, exciting programmatic model of the founder's era may have become old news. The sector the founder entered may have changed and the prescription for success may look different as well. For instance, three decades ago the mainstream theological seminaries were well-established, secure institutions needing charismatic theological figures. Today, with mainstream faiths showing little growth and even decline, the practical skills of fundraising and managing in a no-growth environment are essential elements of the new theological seminary presidents. Yesterday's founders and long-serving presidents could not succeed on their old skill set alone today.

In this way founders are very similar to charismatic leaders. The latter tend to define leadership as a hub-and-spoke model, with themselves as the hub. While this model may fit their personal style, it leaves the organization with an unusually gaping hole when they depart. The founder's excess of personal influence and social capital cannot be replaced, and if they have not taken care to build systems, the organization that represents their life work can be threatened.

WHAT FOUNDERS CAN DO

When a founder chooses comfort over organizational well-being, that situation has to change. Complacency can threaten the long-term viability of the entity that the founder worked so hard to establish. Founders may be operating with an established set of personal behavior patterns that are so ingrained they may no longer be aware of them.

1. **Own up to the problem.**

   It's important for founders to admit when they see the signs that they're not keeping up with the external environment the way they used to. Options include finding a trusted board member, staff member, or consultant who can provide honest feedback.

2. **Commit to self-examination.**

   Look at motives, sources of job satisfaction, and personal preferences and skills. This will help the founder figure out if she is the right person to lead the organization through the next phase of its growth. Some founders may decide that their organizations need new leaders — or that their relationships to their organizations need to change.

WHAT BOARD MEMBERS CAN DO

Board members are in a difficult position because it's hard for most to judge the extent to which the entity is failing to maintain its strategic position.

1. **Take advantage of hindsight.**

   Board members should steep themselves in the history of the organization, especially the founder's role in it.

2. **Notice where the path diverged.**

   With some study of the history of the organization, board members will probably be able to see a point at which the founder's choices took the organization on a different path than what the environment seemed to be demanding.

3. **Seek comparisons.**

   If board members notice that organizations that started after theirs are now thriving and growing while their organization seems to be coasting, there is a good chance that the founder/chief executive either isn't aware of the extent to which her personal preferences have overridden sound strategic decisions, or she is aware and doesn't know what to do about it.

4. Engage the founder.

Board members should approach her respectfully and in a variety of ways to clarify the situation and seek a solution. The board has the ultimate responsibility for the organization.

WHEN THE FOUNDER WANTS GROWTH AT ALL COSTS

Sometimes a founder attempts to grow the organization at any cost. She overbuilds in comparison to the mission and the logical size of the service area. The fundamental story is the same: The founder misreads or ignores the signals from her environment and uses the unique social and political capital gained during the founding of the organization to cement the strategy — but the results are very different.

Even nonprofits respond to the dictates of the market economy. Ultimately, it's the amount and type of revenue flowing into the organization that determine what it is able to do, and that revenue in turn is driven by the needs of philanthropic organizations, individual donors, government funders, and consumers. The nature of the revenue provides a kind of feedback on the founder's ambitions: A growing market signals a desires for more, while a flat or stunted market expresses disinterest by not producing more than a certain amount of revenue no matter how heroic the development effort.

The founder with an outsized appetite for growth faces a central dilemma. On the one hand, she wants to create a large engine of social change. On the other hand, the environment is functioning more along the lines of a motor scooter. This kind of founder will always deal with the imbalance by seeking new and different revenue sources rather than scaling back her ambitions, and that becomes the source of a simmering internal tension.

HOW THE FOUNDER CAN CAUSE MISSION CREEP

When the strategic environment only provides resources for a small effort, the natural response will be small organizations. Niche art museums are small not because of anything about the art itself but because the market in the form of donors and patrons only provides resources for a small collection. This is what it means to have consistency between mission and strategy.

The founder with big ambitions breaks this linkage at the strategy step by accepting the mission but broadening the strategy — known in the nonprofit vernacular as *mission creep*. The organization chases money without giving much thought to how it all fits together. Taken to an extreme, mission creep turns the original mission statement into an archeological artifact — interesting, but of no real bearing on today's reality.

Mission creep is overdiagnosed, especially by those with incomplete knowledge of the organization. It is easy for the casual observer to conclude that an organization is more interested in money than mission because mission is often stated broadly and because the outsider is often not privy to the strategy. What they see as mission creep may be nothing more than an indirect way of accomplishing the mission, not a distraction from it. Moreover, scale makes mission creep insidious. A minor deviation from mission can be tolerated, especially in a large and growing organization. An extreme focus on growth for its own sake only becomes a problem when efforts unrelated to mission take up a significant portion of time and resources. This is exactly what a zealous, internationally oriented founder threatens in Case Study 4, "Growth by Lurches" (see page 25).

HOW STAFF AND BOARD RESPOND

When the environment demands one thing and the founder responds with another, using a founder's unique leverage to quash dissent or sway a weak board, the predictable result is confusion. Staff members will quietly say things like "we don't know what we're all about," or "every month we change direction," or "we're just running after money." These are signs of trouble in the staff ranks because they suggest that the single-minded focus on the mission, the one thing that should unequivocally distinguish a nonprofit from a for-profit, is being obscured.

For their part board members probably feel the same way. They can begin to lose interest in the organization, rationalizing that it is growing well beyond the neatly self-contained unit for which they originally signed on. Those who are there because of their relationship to the founder (probably quite a few fit this description in the beginning) may see the problem but prefer to take their cues from the founder. Others, since they experience it infrequently, are less likely to recognize the problem. In some circumstances they may even feel that what they are seeing is a sign of vibrancy and enthusiasm. In short, the board of directors frequently is fragmented, tiring, and/or unable to confront the truth about what is happening.

A SUBTLE INCREASE IN CONTROL

When the founder pushes the boundaries of the mission beyond where they should stretch, the organization is falling more and more under the founder's sole control. It moves beyond being an entity designed to serve some kind of societal or economic dysfunction to an entity that exists largely for the purposes of the founder. This is where the functional boundaries between a nonprofit public charity and a privately held corporation are blurred. Some say this type of founder "acts as though she thinks this is her own business." The founder profiled in Case Study 5, "The Ties That Bind," in chapter 4 (see page 33) would very likely have provoked those comments in her own organization.

Even if the founder does not exercise undue control over the organization, her position as chief program and funds developer gives her tremendous control. The time it takes to conceive, design, and implement a new service is when the founder cements her hold on this new offering. It is likely to be quite a while before anyone else in the organization exceeds her institutional knowledge — and meanwhile, she has created a de facto control mechanism.

This type of founder also takes advantage of a less obvious source of power to maintain control of the organization. When each new program or service goes beyond the original mission, it becomes one of a kind in the organization. When the founder adds many new one-of-a-kind services there is a tendency for them to stay within their own defined areas since they have so little in common with the other programs and services. Each new silo compounds the essential problem — the sum of the parts adds up to more than the whole. But being the chief common thread among all the silos boosts the founder's power over them significantly. This survival strategy is common, but largely unnoticed.

OTHER OUTCOMES OF GROWTH FOR GROWTH'S SAKE

To be sure, not all growth-at-all-costs founders keep control of their growing enterprise. Some build the entity to such a point that it exceeds either their personal comfort level or their management ability. The first indicator is often a noticeable decline in quality. With so many different, incompatible things going on, maintaining a core level of service quality becomes difficult if not impossible. One founder of such a rapidly growing organization ultimately lost control of the entire organization when funders and individual donors began questioning his ability to manage such a diverse group of services.

Sometimes the entity led by this type of founder thrives by becoming adept at basic administrative tasks. Here, the chief executive delegates almost total quality responsibility to the leaders of the service silos and concentrates instead on providing back-room support. This is a rare development in the nonprofit world, but it does happen, and it illustrates one pathway to success for this type of founder. For example, during the heyday of direct federal funding for social and economic development in the late 1970s and early 1980s, one nonprofit founder effectively positioned her organization as virtually the sole gateway for federal funds for the region. When a good part of the funding eventually disappeared as a result of federal cutbacks, she simply reduced the scale of the organization to concentrate successfully on just the one or two services that survived the cutbacks.

WHAT FOUNDERS CAN DO

Founders who manage by the flavor-of-the-month may find it exciting, but it's no fun for the board and staff, who know that they're in a constant game of catch-up that they can't possibly win. These kinds of founders may be good at identifying opportunities and capitalizing on them, but in doing so they stretch the mission in so many ways so many times that it's almost unrecognizable — and run the risk that what they've built will become unsustainable. The staff and board may already be grumbling, although many of them are so loyal that they won't say anything until it's too late.

1. **Stop growing for the sake of growing.**

   Constant growth offers many advantages for an organization, but growth for its own sake can actually weaken a nonprofit.

2. **Take a clear-eyed analytical look at what's been built.**

   Some services may have to be closed or reduced because they are far afield of the mission. Unrelated programs drain time, money, and energy.

3. **Think ahead.**

   Make sure all the growth in the future is logical and as seamless as possible. Start with the mission and then make sure the strategy supports it, bringing on new programs and services only if they support the strategy.

WHAT BOARD MEMBERS CAN DO

Often, when something doesn't feel right, it isn't. When board members have strong misgivings, they shouldn't ignore them. They should listen to them and examine them in detail.

1. **Probe with questions.**

   What is gained by this constant focus on growth? Who gains from it? How do most staff members react to this strategy? Asking these questions doesn't qualify as micromanaging as long as it is focused on the organization as a whole. It's a form of intelligence gathering, a way to look for cues and clues.

2. **Check for a disconnect.**

   If board members find one exists between the founder and the rest of the organization, it's time for organizational self-assessment. Does the board understand the mission? Is there a strategy? If the board has to work hard to discern the strategy, that's a clue. If it seems inscrutable or downright opaque, that's another clue. It should be possible to draw a straight line between strategy and programs. Board members should also reflect on the circumstances that lead them to the situation. The board has an important role in planning and evaluation, and should take care not to become disengaged in these important matters.

3. **Confront the founder.**

   If it's a stretch to connect all program offerings with the mission, then it's time to speak with the only person who can approach that stretch head-on. It must be a discussion about how — not whether — to fix the problem. Mission creep can hurt an organization in many ways, so the discussion is not optional. There are many ways to end mission creep, and most will involve unhappiness on someone's part, most likely the founder's. But it's important that the board stay firm. Expansion for the wrong reasons is never a wise strategy.

~ Case Study 3 ~

WHEN THE FOUNDER CAN'T LET GO

When a nonprofit's founders consistently resist board members' suggestions, board membership often resembles a revolving door until a change in leadership occurs. Will Sally and Jean see the handwriting on the wall before it is too late to rescue the organization they founded?

Education evaluator Sally Tremont and classroom teacher Jean Sprague co-founded a public school for autistic children many years ago at a time when the traditional public system was doing little to provide for children with special needs. A new board member, Annabelle Addison, had heard about the school before she joined the board, but she didn't know any of its students. She was unaware that most members were new to the board or that the majority of those who had served — parents, mainly — had been dismissed.

Jean had pretty much been running the programs single-handedly since the beginning, but it was unclear what Sally did, even though she carried the title of chief executive. Sally acted like the boss during the board meetings, but at other times she appeared to be apathetic.

Annabelle found that the board members' opinions were largely irrelevant. Sally seemed to consider the board a formality. It was practically impossible to obtain the data needed to have a substantive discussion. Whenever Jean tried to speak up, Sally shot her a look that said, "Be quiet."

The board sensed it was time for a change, so the chair found a way to bring up the subject of succession, since the founders were approaching retirement age. Sally made it clear that if the board expected one or both of them to step down, she thought they were entitled to pensions equal to what they would have received had they remained in the public school setting.

They all agreed to work together to outline a transition process with the understanding that a new chief executive would be recruited in the near term; they sidestepped the pension issue. At the next board meeting Annabelle led the board through a planning exercise, and before she figured out what was happening the board was suggesting that she become the next chief executive. Annabelle had a strong financial background and was meticulous. Knowing that she would at last have access to data that would help her and the board make good decisions, she accepted the challenge with enthusiasm.

Annabelle immediately initiated a new strategic planning process among board members that included ideas for raising additional funds. More than anything, she hoped the group would soon function as a governing board rather than a rubber-stamping board. She also began to bring back a long list of disaffected individuals, reaching out to everyone she could and saying "thank you" constantly. Her efforts paid off, and before long the organization was raising more financial support than ever before.

Sally and Jean were retained as consultants during the transition period, even though in Annabelle's view this was not necessary. They were still around at the end of her second year, when Sally addressed Annabelle as her "associate" in front of a member of the board. Annabelle later learned that Sally had approached the board, declaring her incompetent as chief executive.

She appealed to the board chair, who said there was nothing she could do to stop Sally's attacks. Annabelle resigned on the spot. Soon afterward, she heard that the board was launching a nationwide search for a new chief executive. The board recruited a big name from a major university who ultimately led the organization in an entirely new direction. Sally and Jean were no longer a part of the picture.

Then a group of parents from the board decided to form their own school. They hired a qualified team of experts to develop a new curriculum and recommend new teaching techniques. This time around they were committed to doing everything right, including the recruitment of a diverse board and the establishment of clear policies for governance and oversight. The school was operating at full capacity in a matter of months.

The school Sally and Jean had founded no longer existed — they had lost their legacy as well as their reputation in the community. They did not receive pensions in the amounts they had requested. And after nearly two decades of collaboration, Sally and Jean were no longer speaking to each other.

Tip for Sally and Jean: *Clarity would have made all the difference.*

Sally and Jean had the makings of a good idea. They identified a population that was being underserved, and they created a good vehicle to serve it. Their eventual downfall was due to unexamined assumptions about the role of a board, about the difference in personal rewards of public schools versus nonprofits, and even about each other. In addition, they failed to make their roles clear to others and probably to themselves as well.

The most important of their miscues, however, was that neither professional truly filled an executive role. Jean managed the programs and Sally did...something else. In the gap between them was the chief executive role. The chief executive of a nonprofit is more than just the chief program person, more than the chief fundraiser, more than the chief operations person, and so on.

Tip for prospective board members: *Do your homework.*

Many free public sites for researching nonprofits are now available on the Internet and in many government offices. Prospective board members should try to have an in-person interview with at least two different current board members, on separate occasions. If previous board members have been dismissed, this may be a yellow flag worth investigating. Prospective board members should expect that boards may want to do an equivalent amount of research on them.

Tip for current board members: *Be critical thinkers.*

Board members should ask themselves why it is so hard to get good information and why the founder or her associates seem to regard board members' roles so negatively. There is a reason, and it probably suggests something about the balance of power in the entity. Who really wants to be a rubber stamp?

Founders usually have strong preconceptions and assumptions. To the degree that they are innovative and forward-looking, it is a positive attribute. But in this case the two founders appear to think there is little difference between public employees' and nonprofit employees' benefits. Most nonprofit retirement plans — if they exist at all — are not nearly as generous as public plans. The fact that the founders think this way represents a fundamental, simmering misconception. The board must learn to be sensitive to this and other major differences in thinking and in expectations.

The odd disconnect between Sally's title and Jean's functional leadership should have prompted some critical thinking on the board's part, as should Annabelle's resignation. The demise of this organization may have been atypical in the extreme, but it emphasizes the strong founder's inherent need for a strong board.

GROWTH BY LURCHES

Missions that are too broad give too much wiggle room to charismatic founders who are fond of chasing the next new idea. The board may not be paying attention, and funders may not yet be asking questions, but a nonprofit indifferent to oversight and accountability cannot escape them indefinitely. What should new board members do to get Jim Sharp and the organization he founded under control?

"Our mission is to make the United States a better place to live," proclaimed Jim Sharp, chief executive and founder of a national nonprofit organization active in the area of environmental policy. The board never questioned the mission's sweeping breadth, so Jim would have been able to justify nearly every new project he initiated if the board had any objections.

Jim viewed board meetings as opportunities to appear at his charismatic best. At every meeting, he expounded enthusiastically upon a new project idea he had developed in response to an environmental issue that had recently appeared in the national news.

Emphasis on future projects left little time for updates on current initiatives, even though many of Jim's projects seemed to encounter problems during the implementation phase. If a board member made an inquiry, Jim was usually able to divert the conversation back to his latest "must do" idea. He seemed to capture the board's attention as he peppered his commentary with the names of influential individuals whose support he promised to enlist. By the time Jim finished his monologue, it was usually time to adjourn to the postmeeting cocktail reception.

In truth, many had joined this board so they could meet and get to know their fellow members who had distinguished themselves professionally and had become part of Jim's extensive network of acquaintances. The conversations that occurred over cocktails were the main reason board members traveled long distances to attend the biannual gatherings; most didn't worry about what the organization actually accomplished. Jim did not ask for more than a nominal annual contribution, so the price was well worth the chance to associate with such an impressive group.

A majority of the board members were at the height of their careers and had not allocated time to nonprofit board service before accepting Jim's invitation to join this board. Two of the newest members, however, were seasoned volunteers in their local communities. They had reviewed the IRS Form 990s and decided after their first drink to pull Jim aside to ask him why the budget had fluctuated so dramatically from year to year. They were about to learn that Jim regularly accommodated funding shortfalls by laying off staff, only to staff up again as funding from new supporters emerged — individuals caught up in the urgency of Jim's appeal who had not thought to ask questions before making a financial commitment.

Tip for new board members: *Build board relationships, get the facts, and begin to instigate a culture change.*

Unfortunately, these concerned board members can't do much immediately. This is a long-term structural matter that will take a while to fix. The starting point is the like-mindedness and shared commitment of the two new board members. Given the weakness of this organization and its governance, two determined people can create major changes. To this end, they should use the cocktail party to network and begin establishing relationships with the other board members.

Tomorrow morning, they should check the mission statement. If Jim is right that the mission of the organization really is to help make the United States a better place to live, then it is way too broad and needs to be rewritten as part of a valid strategy and work planning process. But there is an equal chance that the mission statement provides more specific guidance than Jim says it does.

Next, they should split up the list of board members and contact every single one, with the stated purpose of trying to get to know their peers. Establishing individual relationships with their peers really should be their primary objective, but a never-stated yet strong secondary objective in these conversations should be to figure out how their colleagues see Jim and the organization. If the two of them are in the majority, the timetable for the work will move up. If they're in the minority, it will take much longer.

This whole effort will take a long time because this is a social board, not a governing board. Its primary reason for existence is the social ties that it facilitates among members. The whole organization, led by Jim, is reactive in nature. It is governed not by a strategy and a work plan but by outside events and developments. A cultural shift needs to happen that includes these components:

- A more focused mission statement or dissemination and adherence to the real one if Jim is not describing the actual mission statement correctly

- A widely accepted strategy

- A plausible work plan for implementing the strategy

- A commitment to take a disciplined approach to governance

- A board member nominating process based on what value the board member can bring to the organization, not their social contacts

- Administrative help, such as an operations director, for Jim

- A functioning personnel evaluation process, starting with the chief executive

Tip for Jim: *Be willing to hold yourself and the board accountable for success.*

Jim's programs may be excellent or deficient, but he'll never know for sure until he involves his board in strategic planning, puts the plan in writing, sticks to it, and most important, evaluates the results. Planning should start with a full board review of the organizational mission.

Jim's constant introduction of new ideas may be an entertaining diversion for the board, but board members won't take him or the organization seriously until he sticks with one program idea long enough to prove it was a good idea in the first place. Charisma alone will not be enough to sustain the semblance of a well-functioning nonprofit organization in the longer term.

Now that the board has recruited several members experienced in nonprofit governance, the board as a whole will most likely begin to function like a true nonprofit board, rather than a social club. The board exists to govern and be involved in oversight, to partner with the chief executive in times of success and support him in times of challenge, and Jim must encourage his board members to fulfill these roles.

Whether or not Jim believes he will continue to be able to find new prospects willing to contribute funds is irrelevant unless his organization takes the time it needs to create and follow a sound strategy. Nonprofits exist to implement worthy programs; fundraising is the means to the end. If there is trouble securing donors for the longer term, it is probably because they're not seeing tangible results.

Jim must respect your staff and value their contributions to the organization's success. Staff layoffs are not the way to balance the budget.

Jim would benefit from the services of an executive coach, as well as an operations director who can help get things under control. For these efforts to be successful, however, he must be willing to look honestly at the situation and empower others to help him become a more successful professional leader and team player.

4.

The Founder's Internal Relationships

To say that founders are individualists is an understatement. Some mysterious combination of nature and nurture endows them with ample quantities of vision, energy, and drive. Why these qualities were channeled into the creation of a nonprofit organization is probably as much of an unknown as where they came from in the first place. In the beginning, that organization is molded virtually unassisted by the founder. And nowhere does the founder exert more influence on the budding organization than by the board she assembles and the people she hires.

THE FOUNDER'S ROLE IN DEVELOPING THE BOARD

Like nonprofits themselves, boards of nonprofits have life cycles. The early stage is always a period of cautious groping for answers and a feeling-out process for the founder and a group that were probably strangers just a little while ago. More important, it is in the DNA of most boards to be supportive of the chief executive. For founders that tendency is magnified. Of course, that is the heart of the potential problem for the founder's board. The founder may be smart, energetic, charismatic, driven, and innovative, but she can still make mistakes. Just as athletes need coaches and actors need directors, chief executives need the counterbalance of a strong board to make them more effective. One of the ways a board gets true strength in this regard is through its ability to think critically. But for the founder's board, critical thinking is usually not high on the to-do list.

Often what is high on the list is cheerleading. Being a founder or being on a founding board is fundamentally an emotional experience. The objective detachment required by critical thinking is the antithesis of emotional engagement, yet it is the source of a board's value to a founder — or any other chief executive. Complicated as it may sound, the founder's main contribution to her board's development is to give it permission to enjoy the ride while maintaining enough distance to let clear-eyed thinking prevail.

A related service the founder can provide her board is encouragement to develop its own identity. A board is a task group, and every task group needs to create pathways of communication and ways of working together to be successful. An effective founder will find ways to help the board develop its own unique perspective on governance independent of the founder. The urge to make the board a personal fan club is strong, but resisting it is the highest service the founder can provide her newborn governing body.

The ability to think critically while still supporting the chief executive allows a board of directors to improve upon the executive's work rather than simply rubber-stamp it. In many ways the board of a nonprofit organization plays an early version of the same role with its executive's initiatives that the outside world will play. Research suggests that over time the best decisions are made by groups, and the vetting that an engaged, critical-thinking board can provide will toughen a proposal and give it a better chance to succeed once exposed to a wider audience.

Finally, the engaged-but-critical board is better equipped to deal with life after the founder. With its own identity apart from the founder secured, it will see that turning point as a large but manageable version of the same critical junctures it has been handling all along.

THE FOUNDER AND THE STAFF

During the initial stages of a nonprofit organization the founder needs to inspire interest and loyalty in potential staff members. She shapes the organization through her initial hires because of the power of her vision. She selects, motivates, and trains them (at least the first group of staff), and this fact alone explains a lot of the founder's enduring influence on personnel matters. The bonds formed at this time are usually very strong because they have to be. Few professional experiences bond people more than holding one's breath for a period of years with the same small group of people to see if the new idea really does work.

There is little reliable connection between the founder's historic role in starting an organization and her pattern of personnel management. Founders can be just as successful at managing people as any successor executive, and they can show the same weaknesses. What is different is that the founder is likely to have a tighter relationship with the first group of staff members than she or any other executive will have with a group of staff again. Case Study 5, "The Ties That Bind" (see page 33), is a good example of this.

To the first cohort of staff the founder imparts intangibles like excitement, enthusiasm, and a sense of possibility. This atmosphere develops in part because the mechanics of service delivery have yet to be worked out, but also because intangibles are what the founder has the most of at this point. With the exception of chapters of national name-brand nonprofit federated organizations with established program models — such as the Boy Scouts of America, MADD, or Family Service America — it is hard to know what really works and what doesn't. But it is possible from the start to get people excited about the new venture. Those first staff members tend to sense quickly that their job is as much about designing the future as it is about getting the job done today.

HOW THE FOUNDER EXERTS INFLUENCE

The founder's initial choice of staff is a combination of psychology and economics. Young people tend to be attracted to start-ups because they offer a unique opportunity to be a part of something important at a time in their lives when this is attractive. A founder's organization will tend to hire young people for a similar reason, and it doesn't hurt that young employees also tend to command lower compensation. Once on board, this initial cadre of young people will be imprinted with both the enthusiasm and the values of the founder. The resulting shared sense of ownership can be strong.

An organization's culture is carried through the stories it spawns. The Salvation Army still proudly tells the story of William Booth's one-word 1910 telegram to his field officers. Stymied by the high cost of the then-new technology of telegraphs, he pondered deeply how to reach everyone with a stirring message at a reasonable cost. In the end he sent each one an inexpensive one-word telegram deeply resonant with meaning: "Others!" Many organizations still look back on a founder's bet-the-farm moment when the future of the entity was at stake and he or she made exactly the right call. In the first generation of a nonprofit, the subjects of those stories are almost certain to be the storytellers themselves, and this proximity provides a punch. Over time the impact will probably fade, but not until the founder departs.

A founder's too-tight control over initial staff can spell trouble if it does not give way to a more professional relationship. Success and growth over time will force this change to occur. But if an organization chooses to remain small (for the right reasons), it will need to be sure that the early-hire model does not apply to staff coming on later.

In some cases the founder's initial staff will go on to create similar organizations, especially if the demand for the type of services is proven to be strong and reliable. This movement happens most readily in the education field, which tends to be locally governed with programs and services built from the ground up. It is hard in institutionally dominated and mature industries such as hospitals and universities, because the major players are already long established and there are so few opportunities for new ventures. Those who stay with the organization eventually carry some of the present-at-the-founding glow that the founder always carries. Used wisely, this status adds to their effectiveness.

WHAT FOUNDERS CAN DO

For different reasons, a large part of the typical nonprofit workforce — and, for different reasons, its board of directors — is relatively transient, bringing value to the organization for a finite period of months or years. Founders can reverse this trend with their ability to create a uniquely exciting place to work and to serve on the board.

1. **Create a culture of employee growth and development.**

   Many organizations say they do this, but founders have to do it just in order to get the organization started. The start-up entity almost unavoidably forces everyone to grow and develop at an unusually high rate. By emphasizing a culture of self-examination and learning, founders can shape the organization for years to come.

2. **Orient staff to the mission, not the founder.**

   The founder's objective should be to create a strong organization, not a founder-focused social group. By focusing on the mission and the consumers, the founder minimizes the risk of the organization being unable to function in her absence.

3. Provide easy access to external training and education.

Inevitably there will be a high degree of internal education and training for board and staff because the early stage of a new organization amounts to extended, self-provided on-the-job-training. Founders can leaven this mixture by insisting on regular exposure to outside peers, ideas, consultants, and experts. This will help limit the tendency to create an overly inwardly focused organization.

WHAT BOARD MEMBERS CAN DO

Being part of the first generation of leadership on a founder's board of directors can be like repairing air conditioners in the Antarctic — it's easy to feel unneeded. Nevertheless, board members in this situation have the same obligations (and opportunities) as those on a non-founder board. They also have a few special ones.

1. Understand and respect founder-staff bonds...

Board members must realize that the bonds with the first staff members will be there before they come on the scene in any meaningful way, and these bonds are an essential part of the founder's early success. Even if board members wanted to change the situation (and why would they, if it works?), they would be hard-pressed to do so.

2. ...but don't be intimidated by those bonds.

Founders tend to be high-energy, focused, and committed people, but they're not infallible. Most nonprofits' single largest expense is their personnel, and sometimes the founders' talents aren't easily transferable to managing that asset. Boards need to support their founders while still holding them accountable for systematized personnel management.

3. Be mindful of the costs of compromise.

The costs of running a professional human resource management operation are far greater than what organizations with fewer than a hundred or so staff can typically afford. If the founder doesn't have the resources to set up such a professional system, the board will need to be constantly vigilant that the personnel management compromises made in the beginning do not get transferred to the eventual entity that gets created.

THE TIES THAT BIND

A chief executive who succeeds a founder often encounters difficulties when the founder remains on the staff and must be "managed." Problems are exacerbated if the board fears the founder might leave in a huff and prompt public outcry. Does founder Joyce Jemmel really want to resign, or is she bluffing to get attention? What is the board chair going to do to restore order?

The Neuroblastoma Foundation (NBF) was founded by college professor Joyce Jemmel five years ago after her young son Chad was diagnosed with the disease, a rare form of pediatric cancer. Determined to do everything she could to address neuroblastoma and ultimately find a cure, Joyce sought out pediatric oncology expert Connor Smith, M.D., and the pair, with the aid of a small staff, raised several million dollars for research and established a support network on behalf of affected families throughout the United States. Dr. Smith served as NBF's medical director and Joyce served as chief executive, calling upon her writing talents and public speaking skills while Smith, as the expert, took the programmatic lead.

Six years after Joyce founded NBF, her son's condition deteriorated and her mother was diagnosed with a debilitating illness. Reluctantly, Joyce resigned as NBF's chief executive. Although the board was concerned that NBF would falter, it also viewed Joyce's decision as an opportunity to make the organization more professional. Gregory Powers, their top candidate for the chief executive position, expressed his concerns to the search committee that Joyce might want to return if her son or mother died.

Several search committee members agreed with Gregory and were reluctant to see Joyce leave. However, the board chair insisted that the transition in leadership would be relatively straightforward. He also was confident that Joyce had the best interests of the organization at heart and that she knew she could not continue to run it with the increasing demands of her family. In the end, a compromise was reached: Gregory would become the new chief executive while Joyce would assume a part-time fundraising role.

Several staff positions were eliminated to leave room for new hires as Gregory decentralized, restructured, and institutionalized new processes and procedures. The remaining staff supported Gregory as their new leader, although they retained a strong, almost familial allegiance to Joyce and felt responsible to her for the organization's continued success.

Gregory continued to initiate and enforce changes — empowering staff to fulfill specific responsibilities (including budgetary responsibilities by project). Then a staff member alerted him that Joyce often went around him when she disliked his decisions and approached staff members directly. Gregory gently confronted Joyce, but this seemed to make matters worse. Not long afterward, he learned that Joyce had begun talking about him to board members and had even criticized him in a public setting.

Shaken, Gregory decided to proceed cautiously. He became increasingly aware that the families of neuroblastoma sufferers were emotionally attached to Joyce, who as the mother of a child with the disease had the credibility Gregory would never have. Most of NBF's board members had children or other young relatives with the neuroblastoma, too, and Joyce's dedication to the cause had become a source of hope for them. Gregory assumed that they were unable to assess her state objectively, and the few who might understand would probably not challenge her.

Gregory decided that the best way to develop his own relationship with the board was to undertake a strategic planning process. The board had a very productive planning session, and, as a result, several new staff members were added to help implement new initiatives. After a few months, board members began to note Gregory's improvements and expressed pleasure with the organization's newfound professionalism.

Joyce, on the other hand, was impossible to manage. She acted as she pleased, refusing to follow new processes and procedures and continuing to go around Gregory, committing significant sums of NBF's resources without his approval, and announcing new, heretofore unplanned strategic initiatives at public gatherings.

One day at a regular staff meeting, Joyce accused those who had served under her leadership of betraying her, and then she announced that she was going to leave NBF. Stunned, but in some ways relieved, Gregory alerted the board chair. When the board chair told Gregory, "NBF cannot afford to have Joyce leave," Gregory asked the board chair to call a special meeting of the board to alert them and to discuss Joyce's future.

It is now one week later, and the board chair has not yet made a move. Gregory is convinced that Joyce threatened to resign knowing that the board would never accept her resignation. He wonders how things can possibly move forward now that Joyce has created such a disruptive atmosphere.

Tip for the board chair: *Recognize that you need to make a choice.*

The board chair guessed wrong about Joyce's reaction to her family health issues and chose Joyce over Gregory when he did not want to accept Joyce's resignation. He sealed it when he started looking for ways to keep her involved with a part-time role. He encased it in concrete when he delayed taking action. He now faces an untenable choice: Continue supporting Joyce and accept that Gregory will either resign or be hobbled, or support Gregory and deal with the complicated fallout of Joyce's public departure. There really is no easy answer to the dilemma, so he should be prepared for a sustained period of disruption.

Underlying these actions is a lot of ambivalence — perfectly understandable given the personalities involved here. But the board chair has to make a choice, then make that choice work. Not choosing is not an option. Even now neither Joyce nor Gregory knows where the board chair stands. All parties need a decision and clarity so they can move on.

Tip for Gregory. *Clear the air.*

Gregory's choices are limited here, and a lot depends on what the board chair wants. He has undoubtedly figured out by now that if the chair had to choose between the two, Joyce would win. The problem is twofold. First, there is no leadership coming from the board chair. Second, the ambiguity is tearing the organization apart. Both situations have to end.

Gregory should confront the chair privately. If the board says it supports Gregory, the chair must accept Joyce's resignation for the sake of the organization. If he won't do this it means he supports Joyce, and Gregory will need to resign — also for the sake of the organization. The choice is stark, unfortunately, but unavoidable. Prediction: Between Joyce, the board chair, and Gregory, at least two of these people won't be here at this time next year. It would be nice to have better news, but at least there will be clarity shortly. The mission deserves nothing less.

5.

Founder Succession

It is difficult to describe a founder's successful process of termination without sounding like a bland recipe card. In theory, the departure of a founder should be no different than any other chief executive's termination process. What makes it trickier, of course, is that the founder is *not* like any other chief executive. The social voltage of being the person who conceived of and built the organization supercharges the atmosphere of the founder's departure, so for everyone's sake it must be handled effectively.

In the best of situations, when the founder and all around her act responsibly and competently, they pass through three stages: planning, acknowledgment, and severance. Sometimes, however, the board must make the difficult decision to fire the founding chief executive. This chapter describes both voluntary and involuntary termination and the work to be done in each stage of these processes. Case Study 6, "A Founder's Luck Runs Out" (see page 44), highlights how agonizing these termination situations can be. Case Study 7, "Management My Way" (see page 46), illustrates the importance of creating a succession plan well before the founder leaves.

WHEN THE FOUNDER DECIDES TO LEAVE

Everyone understands that a successful end to a chief executive's tenure must be carefully planned. The chief executive usually has unique personal needs involving timing, financial arrangements, and work management that she must shape into a coherent plan. The chief executive position is intended to have the longest time horizon of anyone in the organization — one measured in years, not days or weeks — so it makes sense that the termination be similarly planned.

Apart from the chief executive's and the organization's logistical and operational needs related to termination, the planning stage is really about succession management. This concept is a relatively new one to many nonprofit boards, perhaps because so many nonprofits have been created in the last few decades that they are just now getting to the point where long-serving chief executives are considering retirement. Ironically, many boards have either formal or informal lines of succession for their officers, to the point where it is possible to know who will be the next president of the board a year or two in advance. Why should the same thing not happen with the chief executive?

For a variety of reasons, many boards do not consider the question of succession until it is directly upon them. This neglect effectively means that the planning process must be compressed into a short period and may therefore be less effective (see the following section on unplanned termination for more details). Still, the logical steps are the same.

1. **Consider the organizational strategy.**

   The board's starting point for any chief executive decision is the organization's strategy for the next several years. What does the nature of the strategy imply for the kind of person that the board should seek? What are the skills and attributes that the person should have?

2. **Make realistic financial projections.**

   The next question to answer is what the board can afford to pay. This is no time to engage in false economy. For the foreseeable future the labor crunch can be expected to extend to qualified chief executives as well as to direct-service employees, and so paying tomorrow's chief executive may very well be more expensive than paying today's, even if today's chief executive is the founder. At the same time, it is important to be realistic about what the organization can truly afford. The board's second bit of hard work lies in crafting the balance.

3. **Think about merging.**

   Some boards should at least consider the option of merging instead of replacing the chief executive. The temptation to simply replace the incumbent is understandable, but in many parts of the nonprofit sector the pace of mergers is now picking up, for very valid strategic reasons. Organizations in mature, established parts of the sector — such as mental health services, day care, or hospitals, just to name a few — would be particularly well advised to consider mergers. In minimal-growth environments, the strength of individual nonprofit service providers becomes very important.

4. **Decide whether to hire a search firm.**

   Recruiting and selecting the new chief executive is rightfully regarded as the most important thing a board will do for its organization. The trade-off between managing the process internally and hiring a recruitment firm is between saving money and saving time. There is no one right way to do it. Larger organizations often delegate at least part of the recruitment process to a firm, while smaller nonprofits' boards often must save money by doing it themselves.

ACKNOWLEDGMENT

The founding chief executive holds a special place in the annals of the organization, and her transition out of the entity must be clear and celebrated. This is the time for a party (or parties!), retrospectives, roasts, special naming ceremonies, and so on. It is the time when the organization looks back on a presumably long and successful leadership phase and gives thanks for the founder's contributions.

But the acknowledgment stage is really about stamping boundaries in everyone's mind, and in the culture. Human beings can tolerate good and bad, but an extended dose of uncertainty and ambiguity is intolerable. The pomp and pageantry of the good-bye may seem self-serving, but it serves a useful purpose by underscoring that the organization is crossing a line. The founder's era is now in the past: We move on to the future.

SEVERANCE

The future should *not* include the founder. As we saw in Case Study 3, "When the Founder Can't Let Go" (see page 22), the lingering presence of the founder almost inevitably weakens his successor and confuses board and staff alike. Again, boundaries are useful, and the founder's permanent absence is one more helpful boundary.

There are two practical dimensions to note here. First, one of the reasons why founders in the nonprofit sector resist moving on is the absence of what are fondly known in the for-profit sector as golden parachutes. In a large for-profit entity, carving out a few hundred thousand (or million) dollars for the chief executive's retirement usually can be accomplished with a minimum strain on the company. The equivalent in the nonprofit sector is simply not possible without risking enormous damage to the charity's standing in the community. There is no way in a nonprofit to replicate the advantages of golden parachutes, but there are ways to compensate with a retirement plan (see page 40).

Second, founders need to be needed. And new chief executives can usually use all the help they can get. It is perfectly reasonable and desirable for the successor to take advantage of the founder's immense institutional knowledge. Ideally this will happen during the successor's transition into the organization. If that is not practical, it could happen immediately after the successor takes over, with the founder serving as a paid consultant. For this arrangement to occur, two principles need to be observed. First, the arrangement should be time limited. No matter how valuable, the founder's usefulness as an information source is finite and should be treated as such. Second, the contact between founder and chief executive should be low-key and preferably occur off-site. Again, boundaries are to be respected.

WHAT FOUNDERS CAN DO

Once off the staff, founders need to separate. Under no circumstances should the founder serve on the board, on an advisory committee, or in any other official or semiofficial body of the entity. Case Study 8, "Strategic Tug of War," on page 48 is a vivid illustration of why this is true. Their physical presence in these settings is confusing and sends the wrong message to everyone. The founder carries huge interpersonal voltage. Moving from the chief executive role to the board simply transfers the location of that voltage and infinitely complicates the successor's task. Founders should strongly consider severing all ties, including board membership, with their organization for at least a year before returning to the mission. The founder had her chance to make an unimpeded mark; her successor needs the same.

1. **Strongly consider severing all ties.**

   This includes board membership. The new executive needs at least a year of total freedom from the past.

2. **Be aware of unintentional symbolic messages.**

   Unintended symbolic messages are easy to send — or to be perceived as sending. While there is no guaranteed way to avoid misinterpretation, the founder should be hypervigilant about it. This is difficult and to some degree unrealistic. Over the years the founder is likely to have developed personal relationships with board and staff members, and a perfectly innocuous lunch with one of these old friends could easily be read the wrong way. The only realistic way to deal with this is to be aware that these misinterpretations can happen and move quickly to quash them when they do occur.

3. **Make the intentions clear.**

Founders can make it clear to their successor that they have no intention of interfering, even unofficially. Encourage the successor to check out disturbing reports from the grapevine directly with them.

WHAT BOARD MEMBERS CAN DO

An organization's greatest asset is usually also its greatest liability. The highly successful founder turns into a potential liability the moment she leaves. Whether the departure is planned or unplanned doesn't matter.

1. **Practice succession thinking.**

We made this term up to signify the kind of work that needs to happen before the more formal practice known as succession planning. Succession thinking means the board of directors is always contemplating the state of the organization's leadership even if the founder's departure isn't imminent. Is there an obvious successor among the executives and managers who report directly to the chief executive? More immediately, is there anyone in the group who is qualified to step into the interim chief executive position if there was a sudden vacancy? If the answer is no, the organization faces a distinct risk. It takes a deliberate effort for the chief executive to prepare someone to take over from her, and there are no shortcuts. Begin planning for a vacancy now, and a sudden opening will never take the board by surprise.

2. **Confirm the organizational strategy.**

If there is not a workable, clearly understood strategy in place for the organization, take steps to do it now. It is virtually impossible to succeed at replacing a founder — at least the first time — without a strategic plan.

3. **Discuss needs and expectations.**

What characteristics should the new chief executive have? What skills and personality traits fit best with the future direction?

4. **Review the retirement plan.**

If there is none, try to start one. Having retirement benefits is the best a nonprofit can do in lieu of generous severance agreements. Consult a qualified benefits planning consultant to begin this process. Be aware that, retirement plan or not, deferred compensation options can be used to build at least a modest retirement nest egg for a departing founder if the planning starts early enough.

WHEN THE FOUNDER LEAVES UNEXPECTEDLY

Not all founder departures are well-planned events. Several of the case studies in this publication resulted — or could have resulted — in an unexpected chief executive vacancy. What then?

The board must act quickly in the event of an unplanned termination, and it needs to appoint an interim chief executive. While an insider often fills this role, temporary chief executives from the outside are often available for hire. Whatever the board decides, it needs to act swiftly.

If a carefully planned process is impossible, the board must improvise skillfully. Any lack of a developed organizational strategy only compounds the difficulty. This situation may be likely, as the factors that keep a board from doing succession planning may also mitigate against planning strategy. The absence of a strategy weakens the chance that hiring the new chief executive will be successful, but it does not doom the process altogether. The board should spend some time *inferring* its strategy, asking itself: "What would our strategy have looked like based on the decisions we have made? How might we decide to alter it at this point?"

This way of going about setting a strategic direction is not recommended, but on the other hand, an explicit strategy process rushed into place after the founder has walked out the door is not optimal either. At that point it is better to improvise an abbreviated process and do it well than to do nothing at all.

Having roughed out a strategic direction, the board can follow the steps in the planning stage, described earlier in this chapter. A board that finds itself suddenly without a chief executive still needs to work through the process of recruiting and selecting a replacement. But the board must do different work in place of the acknowledgment phase. Here, the boundaries have drawn themselves, so the incoming chief executive must be selected and groomed accordingly for success.

The board in this situation would do well to consider a few pertinent realities. Potential chief executive candidates are usually attuned to the executive marketplace and may very well know — or could easily find out — about the organization's struggles. An unplanned chief executive departure for any reason rarely resonates in the marketplace in favor of the employer. This problem will need to be handled during the hiring process. If the organization is desperate, this fact will also be known and will weaken its leverage with hard-bargaining candidates. Finally, delays or equivocation in filling the position can discourage staff members and motivate them to leave what they may perceive as a damaged workplace.

WHAT BOARD MEMBERS CAN DO

The inescapable truth is that board members must extend themselves on behalf of the entire organization. If it's any comfort, this period will probably be relatively short, even while its effect will be long term.

1. **Make a plan.**

   It doesn't have to be perfect — and it probably won't be — but it does have to take into account all the factors the board is dealing with right now.

2. **Appoint an interim executive.**

   Give the interim executive clear instructions about what to do and for approximately how long.

3. **Build confidence and trust.**

   The board should hand out liberal doses of reassurance to staff and to itself, and board members should have enough contact with the staff to get information and seek feedback. This is one time when board-staff contact doesn't count as micromanaging.

FIRING THE FOUNDING CHIEF EXECUTIVE

Letting the founder go is always one of the toughest jobs the board has to do. But if it has to be done the board can take comfort in the realization that its loyalty is to the organization, not any one individual.

WHAT BOARD MEMBERS CAN DO

The best practices of human resource management apply to founder terminations, with perhaps a bit more intensity and a different emphasis.

1. **Build the case.**

   Save for rare instances such as documented criminal behavior, founder terminations should never be suggested and accepted at once, such as in a board meeting. Instead, discuss the details in an executive session. Bring the full board together, present the case, and allow all board members to express their point of view or personal feelings about the situation. Create a safe environment where nobody feels uncomfortable about criticizing the founder's performance. Make sure the founder hears the board's concern and gets a chance to improve or correct a situation.

2. **Get a legal review.**

   Document poor performance, significant events, conversations, and previous communications. Check with legal counsel to understand all the caveats and good practices in employment law to protect the organization. Never fire a chief executive without explicit legal support.

3. **Be sure to follow established processes and procedures for termination.**

   Just because it's the founder doesn't mean the process should be ignored. Never allow the decision to be a surprise to the founder — except when dealing with criminal or unethical behavior. Be direct, fair, and professional. Make sure the founder truly understands the reasons that lead to this meeting.

4. **Allow for a resignation.**

   It is in everyone's interests to save face.

5. **Communicate with staff.**

   Be considerate and discuss with the founder how the decision will be communicated to staff and other constituents. The board chair assumes responsibility for internal and external communication.

6. **Communicate about the change with the outside world without waiting for someone to ask.**

7. **Provide for an interim Chief Executive.**

A FOUNDER'S LUCK RUNS OUT

Founders cannot continue to rely upon "beginner's luck" as the nonprofit grows. Does Bill Smith have the courage to admit that the nonprofit he founded may have outgrown his capabilities to lead it effectively? How can board members be supportive of Bill and, at the same time, address the nonprofit's evolving needs?

Bill Smith is founder and chief executive of a nonprofit that administers what used to be the most popular after-school programs in the state. An out-of-work widower with two children in elementary school, Bill started the nonprofit at a time when there were few other after-school options, initially offering one program to a small group in his home and eventually running multiple programs at five sites with the assistance of a talented, professional staff.

Bill had a knack for attracting hard-working, dedicated staff members. In fact, the organization had grown so much in the 15 years since it was established that Bill wasn't really certain what the staff was — or should be — doing. At the same time, he was not particularly interested in keeping pace with the latest developments in after-school education. He had a good idea at the beginning and had been riding the crest of the wave ever since.

Bill was able to garner significant support from one of the state's wealthiest private foundations after only several years of operations. A quiet, understated man with an unassuming personality, Bill had simply been in the right place at the right time.

In truth, Bill felt unsure of himself and his ability to lead the organization he founded. Occasionally he would remark with a smile that he was "just an ordinary guy." This quality irritated some of the staff, but others felt sorry for him and usually found a way to make up for his deficiencies.

Most board members seemed to want to help Bill, too. Many who had been around for years had a stake in the organization's continued success and equated this success with Bill's ongoing involvement. A few, though, were beginning to think it might be time for Bill to move on. Competing programs had sprung up all over the state, putting several of the sites in jeopardy. In addition, the foundation that had provided support for over a decade had pulled back and was about to make the last payment on a final three-year pledge.

Bill realized the organization needed to find the funds to fill the gap, but he didn't want to face it. He had managed just fine all these years, without worrying about funding. He hired a director of development, but she resigned as soon as she realized Bill wasn't about to be involved in fundraising, and he didn't want her to bother the board members with it, either.

Beneath his optimistic façade, Bill was beginning to feel desperate. He thought about resigning, but he didn't know what else he could do to make a living.

Tip for Bill: *Move on.*

Many founders may see themselves in this story. Bill is quickly approaching an inevitable conclusion: It's time for him to rethink his role, and it's better for him to make the decision than to have it forced on him.

Deep in his heart he probably knows that it's time. In the beginning there was a happy convergence of the right person, the right idea, and the right time. Now it's still the right time and the right idea, but Bill is no longer the right person. No shame in that — but there is shame in denying it and refusing to deal with it.

Bill needs to do two things right now. First, he must give some deep thought to what he wants to do with the rest of his life. He may very well not want to run another nonprofit. Fair enough. There are thousands of other options. If introspection doesn't suit Bill, he might get professional job counseling. Next, Bill has to realize that he's built up a network of professional contacts over the years that is pure gold. He should pick two or three people that he can trust and confide in them that he's looking for a new gig. Bill's stock with them is probably so high that they'll immediately start thinking of ways to help.

Finally, Bill should turn the board members into his allies by letting them know what he's been thinking and telling them he wants to handle things in a dignified way. The board will appreciate his candor, and everyone can work together to ensure a smooth transition.

Tip for the board: *Support Bill with honesty.*

The board members know that Bill has talent, and they know his strengths. It is worth a confidential conversation with him to find out what he's thinking. It should be low key, sincere, and done with complete discretion. If Bill is no longer the right choice for the organization, then it is important to send him off tactfully and respectfully.

MANAGEMENT MY WAY

Founders who have had successful careers in the for-profit sector often assume they can employ precisely the same tactics in managing their nonprofits. How can Sam Champlain make a meaningful contribution as his nonprofit matures and learn to respect the roles of others, including the board?

When Founder/Chief Executive Sam Champlain chased away an accomplished program manager by micromanaging him and then frustrated the next person with highly inconsistent behavior, the board's executive committee decided it was time to have another chat with Sam about his management style. Although Sam had been an award-winning sales representative in the for-profit sector before founding his current organization, he had a reputation for not delegating and for taking sole credit for every successful initiative. The board realized that if Sam continued to insist on running the organization as if it were a one-man show, the nonprofit would flounder and eventually cease to exist.

Thus, the board was paying closer attention to how the new director of development was faring. She had set up board and staff teams to meet with prospects and, as good fundraising practice suggested, insisted that the results of all meetings be documented. However, Sam refused to work in teams, preferring to meet independently with whomever he wanted, whenever he wanted — the same way he'd been raising money for years. Sam didn't feel obligated to report back to the director of development on the results of his meetings, either. Once, when the director of development telephoned a major prospect to schedule a meeting, the prospect expressed displeasure with what he perceived to be her incompetence. Sam had been there the day before her call.

The executive committee also knew it must consider a successor because Sam, already in his mid-70s, had recently suffered a major heart attack. Apprised of their intentions and under pressure to comply with their wishes, Sam surprised the board at its most recent meeting by introducing Henry, a young man he presented as his ideal successor. Henry was highly qualified, according to Sam, although his resume lacked the proper experience and he constantly looked to Sam for reassurance during the meeting.

Tip for the board: *Regain control.*

There are so many worrisome things going on here that it's hard to count. Often it's hard to recognize patterns in a small organization, but not here. The essence of the problem is that Sam has the board boxed in. He just blindsided board members with an inappropriate choice to be his successor; he brushed off the executive committee when it tried to talk to him about his management style; and he's causing high turnover among staff. Plus, Sam's behavior undermines his fundraising prowess, and it may actually jeopardize established donor relationships.

The board should show Sam that these well-established patterns of interference cannot continue if the organization is to survive. Things have gone too far. Sam exhibited a lack of understanding of his role when he crossed the line and tried to appoint his own successor. Maybe Henry has skills that can be useful for another role in the organization, but he shouldn't be Sam's successor. The board must make that decision, not Sam.

Sam needs to work on his boundaries with staff as well. A board member he respects should engage him in a series of discussions about how to recognize and respect the differences in his roles and responsibilities and those of his staff. Creating an office manual with written processes and procedures would be a useful tool, too. Sam needs to know that the board is serious about this. It might also consider hiring someone to help Sam, such as a strong chief operating officer who knows this field and won't be easily intimidated.

Finally, the board needs to take control of the long-term future of the organization. Devising a succession plan would be a great place to start.

Tip for Sam: *Channel your passions while respecting the team.*

Sam needs to realize that he's a salesman, not a manager. That may not be bad news. There's a lot of similarity between a successful nonprofit fundraiser and a successful salesman. One sells hope, and the other sells product.

People with Sam's background often look back fondly on their days as sales representatives. Instead of dwelling on internal political battles with the clowns in marketing and the bumblers in finance, they probably most remember the thrill of the win and the bonuses and rewards. Sam may have lived for the days when last month's numbers were released and he was at the top of the sales list — again.

Sam needs to position himself so that he can do what he does best — raise funds. To do so, he needs to work well with others, including the director of development. Right now Sam operates as though he is the only member of his organization, but with written descriptions of staff roles and responsibilities, he will come to understand everyone's unique role, including his. Being a sales rep is one of the last bastions of individualism. Being a chief executive requires working as part of a team. Sam will need a lot of help and support from the board as he prepares to channel his passion and energy in new ways in the time he remains with the organization.

~ Case Study 8 ~

STRATEGIC TUG OF WAR

Founders who step down from their day-to-day responsibilities but remain on the board sometimes feel competitive with their chief executive successors. Feelings of entitlement may cause founders to re-exert their influence, leaving in their wake a dismayed successor and a dumbfounded board. What can be done about Vanessa Hatfield's new idea? What actions must be taken, and by whom?

Vanessa Hatfield, the dignified founder of a nonprofit organization that provides educational programs in the performing arts to disadvantaged inner-city teens, piloted her unique program idea decades ago in London's East End as an experiment. An accomplished British actress, she later met and married a successful American business executive and long-standing member of the affluent suburban community in which they now live.

Years later, as the couple's children grew up and went off to college, the founder decided to revive the defunct programs by establishing a 501(c)(3) nonprofit organization, recruiting neighbors, social contacts, and other friends to serve as board members. She worked as a volunteer chief executive for a number of years, and the organization thrived.

Eventually the group was able to garner sufficient support to cover the salary of an experienced professional chief executive, and Brenda was hired. Vanessa decided it would be best to limit her activities to board membership while Brenda hired a staff person to oversee the programs; Brenda served on the board in an ex officio capacity. Soon Brenda had secured a major grant from the National Endowment for the Arts (NEA) to replicate the programs in selected communities throughout the country.

Vanessa and her husband, now retired, traveled to Europe frequently. She reconnected with her actor friends, discussing with several the possibility of establishing branches of the U.S.-based nonprofit in London, Paris, and Budapest. At the first board meeting after her return to the United States, the founder introduced the idea as a *fait accompli* and offered to travel to these cities herself — at the nonprofit's expense — to help them get things started.

The board was dumbfounded. No one challenged Vanessa, and Brenda was incredulous. She felt that she couldn't possibly manage the organization's local programs and a complex NEA grant project while simultaneously raising the funds required to support the founder's activities in Europe. Furthermore, she wasn't sure that working in Europe was the best choice for the organization at this time. Moreover, when she accepted the position, it was her understanding that the founder was going to step back from program management. The most troubling aspect of the conversation, however, was that no one on the board spoke up in disagreement.

Tip for Brenda: *Apply the brakes, then focus on the future.*

Since no one on the board has spoken up against this out-of-the-blue idea, the chief executive needs to slow things down. She should thank the founder for her offer and tell the truth: This is a big idea (London! Paris!), it's hard enough to focus on local programs, and the chief executive needs time to work through the implications. Then Brenda needs to kill the idea quietly by approaching board members individually.

Over the next several months, Brenda should work with the board to instigate a planning process. Only with a widely understood strategy can this idea be properly evaluated, and the organization doesn't have one. Vanessa's suggestion is not inherently outlandish or inappropriate, apart from the obvious self-interest involved in gaining paid trips back home. It may even make a great deal of sense. But if the organization has only recently settled into its programming and has not even contemplated international expansion, this proposal is a distraction.

Tip for the board: *Strengthen your governance skills.*

Besides planning, another way to focus on the future is to strengthen the board. The silence suggests that board members are cowed or inattentive. If they aren't strong enough to develop themselves, Brenda must help. Tactics could range from providing board member training and development, to term limits, to replacing board members with more effective leaders. Ultimately, the board needs to have a capacity to govern, develop, and manage its membership independently of both the founder and the chief executive.

6.

From One Founder's Success Story, Wisdom for Other Founders

The Student Conservation Association is the rare story of a nonprofit founder who found a way to stay involved with the organization she founded, even though her role has changed significantly. The founder has wisely let the organization grow and develop, even if it has become greater than she ever envisioned. In this closing case study, Liz Cushman Titus Putnam shares reflections on being — and remaining — a successful founder.

The Student Conservation Association (SCA) was founded in 1957 by Liz Cushman Titus Putnam, a young woman with a vision of young adults helping to conserve America's national parks. Fifty years and 50,000 alumni later, SCA's programs now address the needs of local, state, and federal public lands, in addition to our national parks and other cultural and natural resources. SCA's definition of "conservation" today includes energy conservation and the impact of climate changes on our natural resources.

In the early days, SCA received financial support from the then-male-dominated National Park Service (NPS). Idealistic and determined to change the world, Liz viewed the fact that the agency was led by men as irrelevant. She remained true to her vision for SCA's programming, and SCA retained its status as an organization serving, yet independent from, the NPS. She attributes her success to a can-do attitude. "I told them that I would do it all — I would make it easy for them to work with SCA."

It is significant that Mary Mar, who later became one of the NPS's renowned bison biologists, was initially unable to get a job with the NPS. They took an active interest in her only after she had completed an SCA internship.

Liz served as chief executive of SCA until 1970, when she stepped down due to an illness. A husband-and-wife team who had been involved with SCA's programs as crew leaders became her successors and, to a large extent, carried out Liz's vision until they moved on to other challenges.

Then the board recognized that if SCA was to continue to mature, the organization would require increasingly professional leadership at both the board and staff levels. The board decided to undertake a formal recruitment process for the organization's third chief executive that yielded a professional leader with experience in running a nonprofit as a business.

The new chief executive guided the board in the establishment of board member roles and responsibilities and term limits, initiated long-range planning, and introduced risk management as a topic for conversation among board and staff members. Over time, he expanded the number and types of SCA programs to emphasize racial diversity and to include young people who were developmentally disabled and hearing impaired. He also established personnel practices for the staff, upgraded donor programs, and built an infrastructure upon which the organization could grow as he expanded the staff from 12 to 40, with selected positions upgraded (the bookkeeper was replaced by a CFO, for example) and consultants called upon as needed.

This chief executive thought it was critical to establish a distinct identity for SCA separate from its founder because he recognized the organization's potential to become known primarily for the strength of its programs rather than as "Liz's nonprofit." He accomplished this critical image-building task by changing the logo, publishing and distributing high-quality annual reports and other printed materials, and cultivating key relationships with the press.

The chief executive had made it clear to Liz as well as to the board that he thought it was necessary for Liz to distance herself from SCA if the initiative was to succeed. As a result, Liz became increasingly less involved, as the chief executive recruited staff members who became part of his new team. Changes like these are often painful for long-standing board or staff as well as for the founder, and SCA was no exception, although the majority of the board supported the chief executive's wishes.

Dale Penny, SCA's current chief executive, explains, "The board brought in the right person to lead that critical stage of organizational growth; it also ended that same professional relationship after living through a series of bad business decisions. SCA's board has consistently been willing to 'right' the organization as it has become necessary."

The board chose a "healer" as its fourth chief executive — a bright, committed leader who re-established a strong relationship with the founder and reconstituted relationships with staff, students, and funders. Longtime staff member Valerie Bailey, who has worked for SCA for 30 years, explains that "re-connecting with Liz was important to everyone, not just because she is the founder, but because of the person she is — a dedicated supporter of SCA's mission." This chief executive was also in a position to benefit from the many organizational changes his predecessor had implemented.

When the fourth chief executive stepped down, he was asked to take a seat on SCA's board. While this action is usually inadvisable, it has worked at SCA because he was a highly respected professional leader with great integrity, strong values, important insights, and an extensive body of SCA knowledge that continues to prove valuable to the board in its work.

Dale admits he was initially hesitant to accept the chief executive position because his predecessor was on the board and the founder was still involved. He has found the former chief executive to be completely supportive, however, and in his view, Liz's active engagement as founding president and a nonvoting board member has been a blessing. "Liz is SCA's ambassador." Dale adds, "Few founders can go through so many organizational phases and remain positive and supportive. Liz has managed to set aside any ego she has for the good of the mission. By sharing the glory as well as the challenges, she has allowed the organization to flourish. Her greatest legacy to SCA will be in enabling it to grow."

Liz offers this advice to other founders:

- **The mission must be stronger than any one person.** The mission pulls people in, and everybody gains — in SCA's case, it is the land, the kids, the partners, the staff, and the supporters. Fifty years later, it's even more important to get young people and the environment working together.

- **Establish and sustain a firm foundation.** A nonprofit organization can survive many changes if its foundation is solid and the founder, the board, and the staff remain committed to accomplishing the mission. This glue holds it all together.

- **Be a team player.** One person does not make an organization. Each person plays an important role. It's all about working together as a team.

- **Bring in the right people at the right time.** New people from the outside bring fresh perspectives not bound by established traditions or previous behaviors. These new people need to work with the board and staff, not just the founder.

- **Be honest with yourself and others, and be ethical.** SCA has survived many transitions because those involved shared the same positive, ethical values.

- **Try not to interfere during periods of change.** The founder cannot be self-centered if she wants the organization to grow and develop. A genuine belief in the cause and mutual respect for everyone's roles should drive the organization and the founder.

- **Roll with it.** There are times of challenge and adversity in any organization. The trick is to roll with the punches and keep your eye on the ball.

- **Let go when the time is right.** Most founders find it difficult to let go but that has to happen in the interest of the organization. I had faith that the new chief executive would make the right decisions for SCA and lead with integrity, so I was comfortable giving him all the space he needed to lead. The board chair helped me develop the role of ambassador for SCA, which I have happily assumed for many years.

Suggested Resources

Alvord, Sarah H., L. David Brown, and Christine W. Letts. "Founders Who Are Effective over Time: Their Characteristics." *Nonprofit Quarterly*, Summer 2006. With the help of examples from seven social entrepreneurship projects the authors are able to paint a picture of a founder with characteristics to keep pace with the organization over decades of growth and recalibration.

Axelrod, Nancy R. *Culture of Inquiry: Healthy Debate in the Boardroom.* Washington, DC: BoardSource, 2007. *Culture of Inquiry* explains how to create a culture within the boardroom that is marked by mutual respect and constructive debate leading to sound and shared decision making. It details how to develop an environment where board members solicit, acknowledge and respectfully listen to different points of view; where they seek more information, question assumptions, and challenge conclusions so that they may advocate for solutions based on analysis. This culture allows board members to voice their concerns before reaching a collective decision, which, once made, is supported by the entire board. It includes tools for creating an environment of trust, for cultivating teamwork, for stimulating dialogue, and for sharing information. Written by one of the preeminent experts in nonprofit governance, this guide shows how to engage and energize board members and make better decisions.

Block, Stephen R. *Why Nonprofits Fail: Overcoming Founder's Syndrome, Fundphobia and Other Obstacles to Success.* San Francisco, CA: Jossey-Bass, 2004. The key to success for a nonprofit manager, including the founders, is to learn to solve problems effectively. Steven Block recommends managers to skip "1st-order solutions" and head toward "2nd-order solutions" that tend to reframe the issue in a different light. He outlines seven common, tough problems and leads the reader to a successful resolution.

Block, Stephen R., and Steven Rosenberg. "Toward an Understanding of Founder's Syndrome: An Assessment of Power and Privilege among Founders of Nonprofit Organizations." *Nonprofit Management & Leadership*, Summer 2002. This empirical research studied a question "Do founders use their position to influence organizational direction?" A survey instrument looked at, among other things, how board meetings are conducted in founder-led organizations, views on who is responsible for the success or failure of the organization, and how often the mission statement is reviewed in these organizations. The bottom line: behaviors and beliefs between founders and nonfounders do differ.

Connolly, Paul M. *Navigating the Organizational Lifecycle: A Capacity-Building Guide for Nonprofit Leaders.* Washington, DC: BoardSource, 2006. Understand, prepare for, and navigate the lifecycle passages and changes experienced by nonprofits. Learn how to assess a nonprofit organization's stage of development in order to align capacities, manage organizational transitions, and anticipate future challenges. Discover strategies for making the case to funders for capacity-building support.

Ingram, Richard T. *Ten Basic Responsibilities of Nonprofit Boards*. Washington, DC: BoardSource, 2003. More than 150,000 board members have already discovered this #1 BoardSource best-seller. This revised edition of *Ten Basic Responsibilities of Nonprofit Boards* by Richard T. Ingram explores the 10 core areas of board responsibility. Share with board members these basic responsibilities, including determining mission and purpose, ensuring effective planning, and participating in fundraising. You'll find that this is an ideal reference for drafting job descriptions, assessing board performance, and orienting board members.

Kaplan, Sheila. "Knowing When to Let Go: Charles Lewis on How a Founder Says Goodbye to Donors and Staff." *Stanford Social Innovation Review,* Spring 2005. A testimony of a successful departure of a founder leaves us with a positive note: Not all exits are painful and disruptive. Charles Lewis, the founder and chief executive of the Center for Public Integrity discusses how he prepared for his stepping down after 15 years at the helm of the organization.

Linnell, Deborah. "Founders and Other Gods." *Nonprofit Quarterly,* Spring 2004. Deborah Linnell discusses how founders of organizations often are the greatest inspiration for us, while at other times they succumb to an Icarus complex and bring down the entire organization with them. To manage organizational growth, we need to understand that different phases in an organization call for different types of leaders; personal growth in leaders is essential; and we need to detect the early signs of the organization moving to a new phase.

Wertheimer, Mindy R. *The Board Chair Handbook, Second Edition*. Washington, DC: BoardSource, 2008. Whether you are a seasoned board chair wanting to brush up and learn something new, an incoming board chair seeking knowledge and skills, or a person considering the possibility of becoming a board chair, this definitive and newly revised guide provides the blueprint for being successful and effective in your leadership role. User friendly and practical, this book focuses on the roles and responsibilities of the board chair position, addresses the all-important work partnership with the organization's chief executive, and outlines the solid communications skills that the board chair's work requires — skills that invite dialogue in a nonjudgmental, respectful atmosphere. Accompanying materials provide sample agendas, letters, and job descriptions to help you do your job effectively.

About the Authors

Thomas A. McLaughlin has been a senior manager of not-for-profit consulting with Grant Thornton LLP since 2001. Before that, Tom spent 11 years as practice leader for the Nonprofit Management Consulting practice at a large national accounting and consulting firm. Tom has nearly 30 years of nonprofit experience as a nonprofit manager, trade association executive, and management consultant.

Among his previous positions, Tom served as an executive with two major Massachusetts social service agencies and as associate director of the Massachusetts Council of Human Service Providers. He is currently on the management faculty at Brandeis University where he teaches mission-based management to MBA students. Tom is a contributing editor for the *Nonprofit Times*, for which he writes a monthly column. He was the first Nonprofit Scholar in Residence at the Isenberg School of Management at the University of Massachusetts/Amherst. Tom also serves on the board of directors of the Massachusetts Council of Human Service Providers and has served on the board of directors of the Make-a-Wish Foundation of Greater Boston and Family Service, Inc. Tom is also a member of the New England Aquarium's Stranded Animal Emergency Response Team.

At Grant Thornton LLP, Tom assists all types of nonprofit clients with strategic projects, including nonprofit mergers and alliances. He is nationally recognized as an expert in nonprofit mergers and alliances, having consulted to nonprofits in over 200 such collaborations. He is also nationally recognized as an expert in nonprofit financial management and organizational restructuring.

Addie Nelson Backlund is an independent consultant who provides services to not-for-profit and nongovernmental organizations in the United States and abroad in strategic planning, development planning, assessment and evaluation, and executive coaching. Her practice has included extensive work with not-for-profit founders and their boards. Addie has fulfilled leadership, management, and development/fundraising roles at the Metropolitan Museum of Art, the Columbia University Graduate School of Business, the Columbia University School of Nursing, the New York Botanical Garden, the EastWest Institute, and the American-Italian Cancer Foundation, where she currently serves as executive director.

Addie holds a Bachelor of Music degree from Northwestern University in Evanston, Ill. and an MBA from the Columbia University Graduate School of Business. She can be reached at a.backlund@att.net or www.addiebacklund.com.